英汉口译教程系列

实用英汉旅游口译

张积模 江美娜 ◎编著

Interpreting for the Future: Tourism

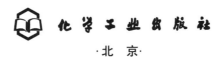

北京

本书由数十年来执教于英语口译教学一线并活跃于大型国际活动现场的两位作者精心编著而成。他们本着实用第一的原则,根据旅游口译最常见的场景将内容划分为 10 个单元,每个单元包括课文 1 和课文 2 两部分。每部分进一步细分为"对话中英互译""短文英译中""短文中译英"三节。在 10 个单元有针对性的口译训练之后,最后的附录部分又列出了作者多年亲身实践积累得来的 16 条宝贵口译对策。

本书章节设置合理,内容科学实用,配标准美式录音,既可以作为大学生口译教材或口译教材的补充材料,也可以作为职业培训教材,还可以作为特定专业学生提高英语听力水平、口语能力的课外读物,可谓一书多用。

图书在版编目(CIP)数据

实用英汉旅游口译/张积模,江美娜编著. —北京:
化学工业出版社,2017.3(2022.1重印)
英汉口译教程系列
ISBN 978-7-122-28974-2

Ⅰ.①实… Ⅱ.①张… ②江… Ⅲ.①旅游-英语-口译-高等职业教育-教材 Ⅳ.①F59

中国版本图书馆 CIP 数据核字(2017)第 019469 号

责任编辑:王丽丽　　　　　　　　　　　装帧设计:史利平
责任校对:宋　玮

出版发行:化学工业出版社(北京市东城区青年湖南街 13 号　邮政编码 100011)
印　　装:北京盛通数码印刷有限公司
710mm×1000mm　1/16　印张 11¼　字数 226 千字　2022 年 1 月北京第 1 版第 4 次印刷

购书咨询:010-64518888　　　　　　　　售后服务:010-64518899
网　　址:http://www.cip.com.cn
凡购买本书,如有缺损质量问题,本社销售中心负责调换。

定　　价:38.00 元　　　　　　　　　　　版权所有　违者必究

前　言

说到外语学习，人们自然会想到翻译。说到翻译，自然会想到口译。说到口译，自然会想到交替传译或同声传译。

随着经济全球化的加速，社会对口译人才的需求越来越大，要求也越来越高。很多外语专业的学生把成为合格的同传译员作为自己追求的最高目标，非英语专业的学生也紧随其后，纷纷加入到口译员的行列中来。然而，现实情况又如何呢？

我国学英语的人数高达几亿，但真正能用英语工作的人并不多，能够作口译的更是少之又少。很多人在从事口译工作，然而称职的没有多少，优秀的就更是寥寥无几。这究竟是什么原因呢？

主要是因为社会上对英语学习本身的误解。大部分人都把英语当成知识来学，把活生生的语言变成了枯燥的语法规则的掌握和单词量的积累，忽视了或者根本没有意识到学英语是一种能力的培养。有很多译员拥有大学英语四、六级证书或专业英语四、八级证书，有的还参加了各种口译证书的培训，可是，就是这样一群精英人士常常连基本的英文自我介绍都做不好，连个简单的名片都写不对。奇怪吗？一点都不奇怪。这是因为四六级也好，专四专八也罢，反映出来的统统是"应试能力"，而口译是"应用能力"的真实体现。一字之差，天壤之别！

现在，大部分高校的英语系都开设了口译课，有硕士点的学校还开设了同声传译。口译教程也是琳琅满目，但良莠不齐，欧式汉语、中式英语充斥着课本，让学习者无所适从。

众所周知，口译不是教出来的，是练出来的。口译能力的培养靠的是时间投入与大量练习，此外，别无他法。笔者根据多年口译教学和口译实践经验，编写了这本口译实用教材。该教材以旅游为主题，这样，既方便了相应领域的口译人员，又方便了口译自学者，可以针对性地反复练习，达到熟能生巧的地步。该书既可以作为大学生口译教材或口译教材的补充材料，又可以作为职业培训教材，还可以作为特定专业学生提高英语听力水平、口语能力的课外读物，可谓一书多用。

本书在编写过程中参考了国内外大量网站的资料，在此一并致谢。由于时间仓促，加上笔者能力有限，疏漏在所难免，欢迎本书使用者不吝金玉，批评指正。

张积模

2016 年 5 月

目录 | Contents

第 1 单元　前往酒店　On the Way to the Hotel　/ 1

第 2 单元　酒店住宿　Check in and Check out　/ 15

第 3 单元　问路指点　Asking for Directions　/ 30

第 4 单元　观光游览　Sight-seeing　/ 44

第 5 单元　饭店就餐　Eating Out　/ 58

第 6 单元　休闲购物　Shopping　/ 71

第 7 单元　出境入境　Entry and Exit　/ 85

第 8 单元　邮政服务　At the Post Office　/ 100

第 9 单元　银行业务　At the Bank　/ 113

第 10 单元　深度旅游　In-depth Travel　/ 127

附录　口译对策　Coping Tactics　/ 142

第1单元

前往酒店

On the Way to the Hotel

# Text A

Section Ⅰ: Dialog

Interpret the following dialog alternatively into English and Chinese.

游客：Hey! Taxi! Over here!

出租车司机：您好。

游客：Hi. Thanks for stopping.

出租车司机：不客气。去哪儿?

游客：Downtown, please.

出租车司机：好的。市区哪儿?

游客：Shangri-La Hotel.

出租车司机：没问题。

游客：Would you please pop the trunk? I'd like to put my bag into it.

出租车司机：好的。我来帮您。好了，放好了。快上来吧。

游客：Thank you. It's very kind of you.

出租车司机：嗯，您从哪儿来?

游客： New York.

出租车司机：欢迎，欢迎。这是您第一次到这儿来吗?

游客：No. This is actually my second visit to Shanghai.

出租车司机：那您对这个城市并不陌生了。

游客：Not really. I came here 10 years ago for a negotiation, and I stayed here for only 3 nights.

出租车司机：10 年前? 那可不短啊! 您也没有机会转转。

游客：No. The Bund is the only place we visited last time.

出租车司机：真可惜! 对了，您对今天的上海印象如何?

游客：I'm deeply impressed. Everything is new here—the airport, the roads, the sights along the way. True. Anything could happen in 10 years' time!

出租车司机：没错。过去 10 年变化太大了，当地人也觉得跟不上节奏呢。

游客：I've heard a lot about Shanghai back home, you know. And I am very excited now because I will see with my own eyes the beauty of this magic place in the next few days.

出租车司机：是的，我从您脸上的表情已经看出来了。

游客：Really? To tell you the truth, I can even hear my own heartbeat.

出租车司机：别激动。嗯，您贵姓?

游客：Clinton.

出租车司机：我们到了。香格里拉。

游客：Oh, so fast. They all say happy time passes quickly. Now I'm convinced. I have an idea, Miss...?

出租车司机：我姓王。

游客：OK, Miss Wang. Could you possibly show me around tomorrow?

出租车司机：好啊。

游客：Great. Come pick me up tomorrow morning at 8 o'clock. I'll meet you up in the lobby. Here's the fare.

出租车司机：谢谢。好好休息。明天早上见。

Section Ⅱ: Passage
Interpret the following passage into Chinese.

Cape Town

Cape Town is the second most populous city in South Africa, after Johannesburg, and the provincial capital and primate city of the Western Cape. As the seat of the National Parliament, it is also the legislative capital of the country. It forms part of the City of Cape Town metropolitan municipality. The city is famous for its harbour, for its natural setting as well as for such well-known landmarks as Table Mountain and Cape Point.

Located on the shore of Table Bay, Cape Town was originally developed by the Dutch East India Company as a victualling station for Dutch ships sailing to East Africa, India, and the Far East. Jan van Riebeeck's arrival on 6 April 1652 established the first permanent European settlement in South Africa. Cape Town quickly outgrew its original purpose as the first European outpost at the Castle of Good Hope, becoming the economic and cultural hub of the Cape Colony. Today it is one of the most multicultural cities in the world, reflecting its role as a major destination for immigrants to South Africa. In 2011, the metropolitan region had an estimated population of 3.74million. The city was named the World Design Capital for 2014 by the International Council of Societies of Industrial Design. In 2014, Cape Town was named the best place in the world to visit by *The New York Times*.

Cape Town has a Mediterranean climate with mild, moderately wet winters and dry, warm summers. Winter lasts from the beginning of June to the end of August. Winter months in the city average a maximum of 18.0℃ and a minimum of 8.5℃. Total annual rainfall in the city averages 515 millimeters. Summer, which lasts from early December to March, is warm and dry with an average maximum of 26.0℃ and a minimum of 16.0℃. Cape Town's average amount of sunshine per year compares favorably with that of Los Angeles and exceeds that of Athens and Madrid.

Cape Town is home to a total of 19 different vegetation types, of which several are completely endemic to the city and occur nowhere else in the world. It is also the only habitat of hundreds of endemic species, and hundreds of others which are threatened. This enormous species diversity is mainly because the city is uniquely located at the convergence point of several different soil types and micro-climates.

The Cape Town region generally, with its Mediterranean climate, extensive coastline, rugged mountain ranges, coastal plains, inland valleys and semi-desert fringes, has much in common with Southern California.

Section Ⅲ: Passage
Interpret the following passage into English.

旅行的益处

很多人都在想，度假到底应该做些什么？我发现，在旅行这个问题上，很多人似乎与我意见不一。我认为，重要的是去看看世界，见见世面，体验一下不同的文化。旅行让我们敞开心胸，接受新事物，用全新的方式体验精彩的生活。

旅行使我们有机会摆脱常规的生活，可以在几个星期内把问题忘得一干二净。旅行可以帮你找到问题的答案，要是没有旅行所带来的空间是很难想象的。我们每个人都有繁忙的日程表，有繁重的工作，有家庭要去照顾。外出度假，一个人也好，和几个朋友一起也罢，可以给你所需要的空间，也许还会让你意识到这些人对你来说有多么重要。俗话说得好：失去方知珍贵。

旅行的另一大好处就是放松。充分享受生活，一个人轻松度过一段时光，想必很好。外出度假能让我们摆脱常规的生活，好好充电。回来后，会感到精力充沛，很高兴又回到原来的日常生活中去。这是减压的好办法，有很多好处，只是很多人不愿意接受而已。

旅行可以增长见识，扩大视野。领略新的习俗、体验不同的生活方式对大脑来说极为有利。旅行让人重新审视人生，尤其是我们自己的生活。旅行可以帮助我们改变自己的习惯，甚至创造新的习惯。发现不同的价值观念、不同的生活方式真的很有趣。

新的经历会让你变得头脑灵活。这一点很重要。回到原先的生活中后，尤其如此。我注意到，经常出去旅游的人不惧变化，而且有能力解决他人避之唯恐不及的问题。

与朋友或家人一起旅行会带来一生的美好回忆。这些回忆将建立一条友情或亲情的纽带，没有任何东西可以将其斩断。旅行让人重新审视这种关系，使其牢不可破。旅行还会让你积累很多好故事，日后可以讲给别人听。你可以创建相册，记录旅行的情况。想起来的时候，可以拿出1小时的时间，看看照片，回顾一下当时的经历。

如果你能抽出一些时间来，我建议你出去走一走，全面体验一下生活。不要等待，不要告诉自己以后会有更好的时间。抓住机会，买张机票，现在就走。等你回来之后，绝对不会后悔。相反，一旦从机场回到家里，你就会马上计划着下一次的旅行。

Section Ⅰ：Dialog

游客：嘿！出租车！这边儿！
出租车司机：Hi.
游客：您好。谢谢。
出租车司机：My pleasure. Where to?
游客：市区。
出租车司机：OK. Whereabouts downtown?
游客：香格里拉酒店。
出租车司机：You got it.
游客：请打开后备厢，我把行李放进去。
出租车司机：No problem. Let me help you. OK. There it goes. Jump in, please.
游客：谢谢。太感谢了。
出租车司机：Well, where are you from?
游客：纽约。
出租车司机：Welcome. Is this the first time for you to be here?
游客：不是。实际上，这是我第二次来到上海。
出租车司机：So you are no stranger to the city.
游客：那倒不是。我10年前来这里谈判，只停留了3个晚上。
出租车司机：10 years ago? That's a long time! And you didn't get a chance to go around.

游客：没有。上次只去了外滩。

出租车司机：What a shame! By the way, what is your impression of Shanghai today?

游客：非常不错。一切都焕然一新——机场、道路，还有沿途的风景，全是新的。是啊，10 年的时间，什么都可能发生啊！

出租车司机：You said it. Great changes have taken place over the past 10 years. Even the locals find themselves slow and out of sync.

游客：您知道，在国内我常常听人们谈起上海。我现在很激动，因为在未来的几天里，我将亲眼目睹这个神奇城市的巨大魅力。

出租车司机：Yeah, I can see that by the expression on your face.

游客：是吗？ 说实话，我现在就可以听见自己心跳的声音。

出租车司机：Chillax, Mr...?

游客：免贵姓克林顿。

出租车司机：Here we are at the hotel. Shangri-La.

游客：噢，真快。都说，欢愉嫌时短。我算是信了。我有个想法。小姐，您怎么称呼？

出租车司机：Wang.

游客：好的，王小姐。您明天能陪我转转吗？

出租车司机：Why not?

游客：太好了。明天早上 8 点来接我。我们在一楼大厅见。这是车费。

出租车司机：Thanks. Have a good rest. See you tomorrow morning.

Section Ⅱ：Passage

开普敦

开普敦是南非人口第二大城市，仅次于约翰内斯堡，是西开普省省会和首要城市。作为国民议会的所在地，开普敦也是南非的立法首都。它是开普敦大都市的一个组成部分。该市因港口、自然环境以及诸如桌山和开普角等地标而闻名。

开普敦位于桌山湾畔，最初是由荷兰东印度公司开发的，目的是为前往东非、印度和远东的荷兰船只提供一个储粮站。1652 年 4 月 6 日，杨·范·里贝克到来，在南非建立了第一个永久性的欧洲殖民地。开普敦很快便超出了原先的用途，即作为欧洲在好望堡的第一个前哨，成为开普殖民地的经济、文化中心。今天，它是世界上多元文化最突出的城市之一，是移民南非的主要目的地。2011 年，大都市地区的人口达到 374 万左右。2014 年，该市被国际工业设计协会评为"世界设计之都"；同年，被《纽约时报》评为世界上"最佳旅游城市"。

开普敦属于地中海气候，冬季温和潮湿，夏季干燥温暖。冬季从6月初开始，一直持续到8月底。冬季城市的平均气温，最高为18.0摄氏度，最低为8.5摄氏度。年均降雨量为515毫米。夏季从12月初开始，一直持续到3月，温暖干燥，平均气温最高为26.0摄氏度，最低为16.0摄氏度。开普敦每年的平均日照时间可以与洛杉矶媲美，超过了雅典和马德里。

开普敦共有19种不同类型的植被，其中一些是该地特有的，世界其他地方难觅踪影。开普敦也是数百个当地特有物种的唯一栖息地。另外，还有几百个濒危物种。此地的物种之所以如此丰富，主要是因为其独特的地理位置。这里集合了几种不同类型的土壤和特点各异的小气候。

总的来说，开普敦地区属于地中海气候，拥有漫长的海岸线、崎岖的山脉、沿海平原、内陆山谷和半沙漠边缘，与南加州有许多共同之处。

Section Ⅲ: Passage

The Benefits of Traveling

Many people ponder what they should do for a vacation and I have realized a lot of people don't seem to share my views about traveling. I believe it's very important to see the world and different cultures. It lets us open our minds to new things and we get to experience life in exiting different ways.

Traveling gives us the opportunity to disconnect from our regular life. You get to forget your problems for a few weeks. It can also help you figure things out that you would not have understood without the distance traveling can give you. We all have crazy schedules, work and a family to take care of. Going away alone or with some friends can give you the distance you need and perhaps even make you realize how important these people are for you. As the saying goes, we never know what we have until we lose it.

Another great benefit is relaxation. It's nice to live life to its fullest and enjoy a stress-free time with yourself. Going on a vacation lets us recharge our "batteries" by disconnecting us from our regular life. When we come back we feel invigorated and we are happy to be back in our day to day routine. It's a very good stress remover that has a lot more to give than most people are willing to accept.

Traveling increases our knowledge and widens our perspective. To view new customs, different ways of living is fantastic for the mind. It gives us a new perspective about life and especially our life. It can help us change some of our habits or even create new ones. Discovering different values and ways to get by in life is really interesting.

New experiences increase our resourcefulness. This is very important for you, especially when you come back to your routine. I have noticed that people who have traveled a lot in life are ready to embrace change and have a natural ability of overcoming problems that others would frown upon.

When traveling with friends or family it creates memories for a lifetime. These memories will create a bond that nothing can erase no matter what happens with the friendship or relationship. It gives a new perspective on the relationship and cements the bond forever. It also gives nice stories to tell people afterwards. You can create photo albums about your trips and when you feel nostalgic you can take an hour of your life and experience the trips again by looking at your pictures.

If you have some time off I suggest you take a trip and experience what life has to offer. Don't wait or tell yourself there will be a better time to go. Take the opportunity and buy your plane ticket right now and leave. When you come back you won't be sorry that you left. On the contrary, you will be thinking of your next trip the second you come back from the airport.

课文 2　Text B

Section Ⅰ: Dialog

Interpret the following dialog alternatively into English and Chinese.

游客: Oh boy, there are so many people! Where is the taxi stand? I got it. Excuse me, sir, are you engaged?

出租车司机: 没有，小姐。您要用车吗?

游客: Yes. Take me to this address, please.

出租车司机: 让我看看。建国饭店。没问题。对了，咱们应该什么时候到?

游客: As soon as possible, because I'm going to meet a very important person there. Can we make it at 10:30?

出租车司机: 我想赶得过去。只要不堵车，就没问题。

游客: Is this the right way? The cabdriver used a different road last time I came, if my memory serves me.

出租车司机: 没错。这条路车不多。那条路正在维护呢。

游客: I see.

出租车司机: 如果您不介意的话，请问，您上次各处转了吗?

游客: No. I came here to attend a one-day business meeting, and I left the day after.

出租车司机：我理解。对商务人士而言，工作总是第一位的。

游客：You may say so. Actually I do want to go around. Where do people go?

出租车司机：您是喜欢自然景观，还是人文景观？

游客：Cultural landscape.

出租车司机：我知道一个好地方，总是人来人往。那就是故宫！

游客：You mean the Forbidden City? I've heard of that before. But I don't know much about it.

出租车司机：实际上，它是明清两朝的皇宫，离今天有590多年了。24位皇帝在里边住过。

游客：24 emperors! That's incredible! I heard that there are altogether 9,999 rooms. Is that true?

出租车司机：那只是传说。事实上，一共有8700多间房子。

游客：Wow, you do know your place well. I have already begun to enjoy my trip. Thank you.

出租车司机：过奖了。随时为您效劳，小姐。嗯，到了。

游客：How much do I owe you?

出租车司机：56元。

游客：Here's 60, and keep the change.

出租车司机：谢谢。祝您在此一切顺利。

游客：Bye.

Section Ⅱ：Passage

Interpret the following passage into Chinese.

Paris

Paris is the capital and most populous city of France. It is situated on the Seine River, in the north of the country, at the heart of the Île-de-France region. Within its administrative limits, the city had 2,243,833 inhabitants in 2010 while its metropolitan area is one of the largest population centres in Europe with more than 12 million inhabitants.

An important settlement for more than two millennia, Paris had become one of Europe's foremost centres of learning and the arts, and was the largest city in the Western world until the turn of the 18th century. Paris was the focal point for many important political events throughout its history, including the French Revolution. Today it is one of the world's leading business and cultural centers, and its influence in politics, education, entertainment, media, science, fashion and the arts all contribute to its status as one of the world's major cities. The city has one of the largest GDPs in the world, 607 billion (US $ 845 billion) as of 2011, and as a result of its high concentration of national and international political, cultural and scientific institutions, is one of the world's leading tourist destinations. The Paris Region hosts the world headquarters of 30 of the Fortune Global 500 companies in several business districts.

Centuries of cultural and political development have brought Paris a variety of museums, theatres, monuments and architectural styles. Many of its masterpieces such as the Louvre and the Arc de Triomphe are iconic buildings, especially its internationally recognized symbol, the Eiffel Tower. Long regarded as an international centre for the arts, works by history's most famous painters can be found in the Louvre, the Musée d'Orsay and its many other museums and galleries.

Paris is a global hub of fashion and has been referred to as the "international capital of style", noted for its haute couture tailoring, its high-end boutiques, and the twice-yearly Paris Fashion Week. It is world renowned for its haute cuisine, attracting many of the world's leading chefs. Many of France's most prestigious universities and Grandes Écoles are in Paris or its suburbs, and France's major newspapers *Le Monde*, *Le Figaro*, *Libération* are based in the city.

The city is a major rail, highway, and air-transport hub. Opened in 1900, the city's subway system, the Paris Métro, serves 5.23 million passengers daily. Paris is the hub of the national road network. So you will find it easy to travel in the city.

Section Ⅲ: Passage
Interpret the following passage into English.

鼓浪屿

鼓浪屿是位于我国南部福建省厦门市沿岸附近的一个岛屿，面积约 2 平方千米。鼓浪屿是 2 万多人的家园，同时也是著名的旅游胜地。

游客从厦门本岛乘轮渡 10 分钟左右可以到达。鼓浪屿岛因众多的海滩、蜿蜒的小巷和风格迥异的建筑而闻名。该岛为国家风景名胜区，位于全省十佳景区之首。

厦门在中国第一次鸦片战争失利以及 1842 的《南京条约》之后成为一个通商口岸，因此，岛上维多利亚时代风格的建筑随处可见。包括英国、法国和日本在内的 13 个国家在此设立了领事馆，建教堂、建医院。1903 年，鼓浪屿正式成为国际租界。1941年，日军占领该岛，一直持续到第二次世界大战结束。岛上居民讲闽南话。

鼓浪屿在厦门殖民地时代是许多西方人的居住地，因此，它因建筑而闻名。同时，它也是我国最大的钢琴博物馆的故乡，于是，便有了"钢琴之岛""钢琴之城"和"音乐之岛"的美称。

鼓浪屿这个名字在汉语里也有其音乐之根。"鼓浪"是"鼓"和"浪"的意思，之所以叫"鼓浪"，是因为浪击礁石，声似擂鼓。而"屿"则是"小岛"的意思。

此外，还有郑成功纪念馆、海底世界、用海外华人引入的植物建成的亚热带花园以及前身为八卦楼的厦门博物馆。

鼓浪屿是行人的天堂，岛上仅有的车辆为为数不多的消防车和电动观光车。其狭窄的街道，与世界各地风格迥异的建筑一起，赋予该岛独特的外观。鼓浪屿被中国国家旅游局列为5A级景区。

鼓浪屿是我国仅有的"步行岛"，它只能通过轮渡连接厦门本岛。汽车也好，自行车也罢，都禁止登岛，这就为河对面熙熙攘攘、车水马龙的厦门本岛另提供了一种选择。不过，近期获批上岛的电动观光车可能会破坏岛上的魅力。货物在坡度很大的小道上靠轮式木车拖运，拉车人是几个身强力壮的男子。

Section Ⅰ: Dialog

游客：天哪，这么多人！ 出租车停靠站在哪儿？ 找到了。先生，您好。您的车有人预订了吗？

出租车司机：No, Miss. Can I help you?

游客：是的。请把我送到这个地方去。

出租车司机：Let me have a look. Jianguo Hotel. Sure thing. By the way, when are we supposed to be there?

游客：越快越好，我要去见一个很重要的人。10点半赶得过去吗？

出租车司机：I think so. We shall be OK if there are no holdups.

游客：这条路对吗？ 如果没有记错的话，上一次我来的时候，司机师傅走的是另一条路。

出租车司机：Yes, Miss. This is the road without much traffic. And that one is currently under maintenance.

游客：明白了。

出租车司机：Did you go around the city last time, if you don't mind?

游客：没有。我来开了一个商务会议，时间只有1天，第2天就离开了。

出租车司机：I understand. For a business person, business always comes first.

游客：可以这么说吧。实际上，我还真想逛逛。哪儿比较热闹？

出租车司机：Do you prefer natural scenery or cultural landscape?

游客：人文景观。

出租车司机：I know a great place. It's always packed with people. The Imperial Palace!

游客：你是说紫禁城？ 以前听说过，只是知道的不多。

出租车司机：It was actually the imperial palaces of the Ming and Qing dynasties. It has a history of more than 600 years. 24 emperors lived there.

游客：24位皇帝！ 真是不可思议！ 听说，故宫里共有9999间房子。是真的吗？

出租车司机：It's just hearsay. In fact, it has over 8,700 rooms.

游客：哇，你对自己的城市真是了如指掌。我已经开始享受我的旅行了。谢谢。

出租车司机：I'm flattered. At your service, Miss. Well, here we are.

游客：车费是多少？

出租车司机：56 yuan.

游客：给您60元，不用找了。

出租车司机：Thank you. Wish you good luck here.

游客：再见。

Section Ⅱ：Passage

巴　黎

巴黎是法国的首都，也是人口最多的城市。它坐落在法国北部，塞纳河畔，位于法兰西岛地区的中央。2010年，辖区人口达到2243833人。其大都市区是欧洲最大的人口聚居地之一，总人口达到1200多万。

巴黎，作为一个重要的定居地，有2000多年的历史，是欧洲最重要的学术中心和艺术中心，直到18世纪，一直是西方最大的城市。巴黎是法国历史上包括法国大革命在内的许多重要政治事件的焦点。今天，它是世界上最重要的商业中心和文化中心之一。它在政治、教育、娱乐、媒体、科学、时尚和艺术方面的影响使其成为世界主要的城市之一。巴黎是世界上国内生产总值最大的城市之一，2011年达到6070亿欧元，即8450亿美元。巴黎聚集了国内外很多政治、文化和科研机构，因此，它也成了世界主要的旅游目的地之一。世界500强的公司有30个在巴黎地区设立总部，分布在几个商业区。

经过几个世纪的政治建设和文化建设，巴黎出现了形形色色的博物馆、剧院、纪念碑以及各种各样的建筑风格。它的许多杰作,如卢浮宫和凯旋门等,已成为标志性的建筑。特别是埃菲尔铁塔,已经成为国际公认的法国的象征。长期以来,法国一直享有国际艺术中心的美誉,历史上最知名的画家的作品都陈列在卢浮宫、奥赛博物馆及其他博物馆和美术馆里。

巴黎是全球时尚的中心,素有"世界风格之都"之称,以高级时装裁剪、高端精品店以及每年 2 次的巴黎时装周而著称。巴黎的美食世界闻名,吸引着许多世界一流的厨师。法国最著名的大学和精英大学大都坐落在巴黎及其周边地区。法国的主要报纸《世界报》《费加罗报》和《解放报》总部也都在巴黎。

巴黎是重要的铁路、公路、空运中心。巴黎的地铁系统——巴黎地铁——于 1900 年投入运营,每天输送乘客 523 万名。巴黎是全国公路网络的枢纽。因此,在巴黎出行非常方便。

Section Ⅲ: Passage

Gulangyu

Gulangyu is an island off the coast of Xiamen, Fujian Province in South China, about 2 km^2 in area. It is home to about 20,000 people and is a famous tourist destination.

Visitors can reach it by ferry from the Xiamen Island in about 10 minutes. The Gulangyu Island is renowned for its beaches and winding lanes and its varied architecture. The island is on China's list of National Scenic Spots and also ranks at the top of the list of the ten most-scenic areas in the province.

Xiamen became a treaty port resulting from China's loss in the First Opium War and the *Treaty of Nanking* in 1842, hence the predominantly Victorian-era style architecture throughout the Gulangyu Island, where 13 countries including Great Britain, France and Japan established consulates, churches, and hospitals. Gulangyu was officially designated an International Settlement in 1903. Japanese occupation of the island began in 1941, and lasted until the end of World War Ⅱ. The Xiamen dialect of Hokkien is spoken on the island.

As a place of residence for Westerners during Xiamen's colonial past, Gulangyu is famous for its architecture and for hosting China's largest piano museum, giving it the nickname of "Piano Island" or "The Town of Pianos" or "The Island of Music". There are over 200 pianos on this island.

The Chinese name also has musical roots, as gu lang which means drum waves, so called because of the sound generated by the ocean waves hitting the reefs. Yu means "islet".

In addition, there is a museum dedicated to Koxinga, Underwater World, a subtropical garden containing plants introduced by overseas Chinese, as well as Xiamen Museum, formerly the Eight Diagrams Tower.

The island of Gulangyu is a pedestrian-only destination, where the only vehicles on the islands are several fire trucks and electric tourist buggies. The narrow streets on the island, together with the architecture of various styles around the world, give the island a unique appearance. The site is classified as an AAAAA scenic area by China National Tourism Administration.

Gulangyu is unique in China as a "traffic-free island". It is connected to the main island of Xiamen only by ferry. Neither cars nor bicycles are allowed, thus providing an alternative to the frenetic Xiamen Island across the river, although the recent introduction of electric tourist buggies may be damaging the island's charm. Freight is pulled on wheeled wooden carts up the often steep lanes by strong teams of men.

第2单元
酒店住宿

Check in and Check out

课文 1　Text A

Section Ⅰ: Dialog

Interpret the following dialog alternatively into English and Chinese.

服务员：Good evening, sir. Can I help you?

客人：我来办理入住手续。

服务员：Do you have a reservation with us, sir?

客人：预订了，今天晚上。

服务员：May I have your name, sir?

客人：艾伦·富兰克林。

服务员：Thank you, sir. Hold on a second. Let me check our reservation record.

客人：好的，不急。

服务员：Oh yes. Here. You are Mr. Allen Franklin from Los Angeles, USA. Am I right, sir?

客人：对。我预订了一间海景房。

服务员：I'm sorry, sir. I was told a few minutes ago that there was a power failure in the room you have reserved. So I can't put you in it.

客人：那……

服务员：Well, there's a double room with a nice view of the sea. Will that be fine with you?

客人：我要考虑一下。

服务员：OK. Take it easy.

客人：我能先看一下房间吗？

服务员：You sure can.

客人：几号房间？

服务员：The bellboy will take the key of your room and bring you there.

客人：好的，谢谢。

服务员：You can leave your suitcase with us, sir, if you like.

客人：好的。

（10分钟后）

服务员：Are you comfortable with the room, sir?

客人：满意。我需要做什么？

服务员：We need your passport, and your credit card. And we need to fill out this form.

客人：给。
服务员：Thanks. Please put your name here, and I'll take care of the rest.
客人：好的，给。
服务员：Thanks. OK, done. Have a nice stay with us, sir. Good night.
客人：晚安。

Section Ⅱ: Passage
Interpret the following passage into Chinese.

Camping for Better Health

With just some basic equipment and a positive attitude, you can camp your way to a healthier lifestyle—and have fun at the same time!

We all know how important cardiovascular exercise is for general health. Hiking is an excellent way to get your heart pumping, and camping near a trailhead makes it easy to increase your hiking mileage. Wake up, roll out of your tent, eat your breakfast, and hit the trail. Most campgrounds have easy access to trails of varying difficulty, so you can tailor your day hikes to your personal fitness level and goals.

What if you are more of a couch potato than a hiker? In fact, the great thing about camping is that you can trick yourself into getting a cardio workout! If you are staying at a developed campground, select a campsite that is furthest from the facilities. This ensures you will have to cover some ground on foot every day. Take routes that require you to walk uphill, maximizing your cardio workout. If you can, choose campsites that are "walk-in", not "drive-up". That way, you'll get to walk back and forth to your vehicle several times as you set up.

Camping is good for your mental health, too. Many of us have stressful lives filled with busy schedules, traffic jams, and ringing telephones. The sights and sounds of nature are soothing and restorative. Sitting in a green forest grove or watching a flock of birds fly by helps your brain reset to a calmer, healthier state. Listening to a babbling brook can lull you into a deep, refreshing sleep. Worries about work fade away as you sit by the campfire and feel the warmth on your skin. Camping gives you a break from your day-to-day life and lets you really relax.

We all know that the better you feel, the better you look. The physical and mental health benefits of camping add up to make a more beautiful you. As you become more physically fit and less mentally stressed, it shows in your body. Camping can help give you that special glow.

Speaking of glow, don't forget to bring adequate lighting when you set out to spend the night in the great outdoors. As part of your gear preparation, make sure you bring a variety of lights with you. A good flashlight is essential. A headlamp is worth its weight in gold when you need both hands free to rummage through your gear bag in the dark. And for sitting around the picnic table playing cards, a battery-powered fluorescent lantern is just the ticket. If you will be gone for an extended period or camping in a particularly remote location, consider investing in a lantern that is powered by a hand crank. It is reassuring to have a light source that will work even if your batteries run out.

With proper preparation and a little planning ahead, camping can play an important role in improving your physical and mental health. So get out there and get camping—just don't forget to turn off the light before you turn in for the night.

Section Ⅲ: Passage
Interpret the following passage into English.

度假胜地（第一部分）

度假胜地是一个休闲娱乐场所，吸引着度假的人和/或观光的人。度假胜地可以是某些地方，可以是城镇，有时也可以是某个公司经营的商业机构。

在北美英语里，"度假胜地"这个字眼目前也用来指设施齐全、自给自足的商业机构，这些机构试图在最大程度上满足在此逗留的游客的需求，如食物、饮料、住宿、体育、娱乐和购物等。这个词也用来指酒店，这类酒店提供一系列便利设施，通常包括娱乐活动、休闲活动。酒店常常成为度假胜地的一大重要特色，密歇根的麦基诺岛大酒店就是如此。度假胜地并不总是指某个公司经营的商业机构，只不过这种机构在20世纪末变得更加普遍而已。

度假村可以分为不同的类别。

自身是度假胜地的城镇，或者旅游或度假构成当地活动重要组成部分的城镇，有时叫作度假小镇。如果是在海边，又叫作海滨度假胜地。内陆度假胜地包括滑雪胜地、山地度假村和温泉小镇等。

岛屿休闲胜地是一座岛屿或一个岛群，其中包含度假村、酒店、餐馆、旅游景点和便利设施等。

海滨度假胜地坐落在海岸。英国的许多海滨小镇已经转向，进军其他娱乐行业，其中一些夜生活非常丰富。电影院和剧院依旧是酒馆、酒吧、餐馆和夜总会的"大本营"。大部分娱乐设施都迎合了当地居民的趣味，海滩在夏季依旧是人们流连忘返的地方。尽管国际旅游使人们远离了英国的海滨小镇，但是，它们也为英国带来了外国游客。结果,许多海滨小镇都成立了外语培训学校,这些学校的学生经常回来度假,有些甚至在此定居。

在欧洲和北美,滑雪胜地指的是滑雪地区的城镇和村庄,其提供的辅助服务包括小旅馆、小木屋、设备租赁、滑雪学校以及运送滑雪者的上山吊椅等。

综合旅游度假区是一个旅游胜地,自身包含了吸引游人的必要能力。也就是说,综合旅游度假区不必离目的地(如城镇、历史遗迹、主题公园等)很近以吸引公众。度假区里的商业机构,如休闲区、风景区、历史遗迹、主题公园、游戏设施或其他旅游景点等,可以与目的地的其他企业一争高下。

因此,综合旅游度假区的另一个特点是,它在度假区内提供食物、饮料、住宿、体育、娱乐和购物设施,客人在整个逗留期间都不需要离开度假区。通常,这些设施的服务质量要比其他酒店或小镇餐馆的质量要高。与这些度假胜地密切相关的是会议场所。这些场所一般都在城市里,那里有特别会议大厅、宽裕的住宿条件以及多种多样的餐饮娱乐。

Section Ⅰ: Dialog

服务员:先生,晚上好。我能为您效劳吗?

客人: I'm here to check in.

服务员:您预订了吗,先生?

客人: Yes. For tonight.

服务员:先生,贵姓?

客人: Allen Franklin.

服务员:谢谢,先生。请稍等,我查一下预订记录。

客人: OK. Take your time.

服务员:嗯,有了,在这儿。您是从美国洛杉矶来的艾伦·富兰克林先生。对吗,先生?

客人: Right. I've booked a room with a view of the sea.

服务员:对不起,先生。几分钟前有人通知我,说您预订的房间突然断电了。所以,没法安排您住那个房间了。

客人: Well...

服务员:嗯,有一个带海景的双人间,您看行吗?

客人: I've got to think about it.

服务员:那好,不着急。

客人: Can I see the room first?

服务员：当然可以。
客人：What is the number of the room?
服务员：服务员会拿着房间钥匙送您过去的。
客人：OK, thanks.
服务员：先生，要是您愿意，您可以把旅行箱先放在我们这里。
客人：Good.
（10分钟后）
服务员：先生，房间您还满意吗？
客人：Yes, I am. What do I have to do?
服务员：我们需要您的护照和信用卡。需要填这张表格。
客人：Here they are.
服务员：谢谢。在这儿签个名。剩下的就交给我好了。
客人：OK. Here it is.
服务员：谢谢。好，行了。先生，祝您在此过得愉快。 晚安。
客人：Good night.

Section Ⅱ：Passage

露营有益健康

带上基本的装备，带着一颗积极的心，你就可以通过露营打造一个更加健康的生活方式，同时获得莫大的乐趣！

我们都知道心血管运动对全身健康有多么重要。徒步旅行是让人心跳加速的很好方式。在小道起点附近露营，很容易增加徒步旅行的里程。醒来吧，从帐篷里爬出来，吃完早饭，然后上路。从露营地出发，大都可以很方便地进入各种各样的小道。所以，你可以根据自己的身体状况以及目标制定1天的行程。

如果你懒得动弹，不愿意徒步旅行怎么办？事实上，露营最大的好处是你可以让自己做一些有氧运动！如果你住在一个设施齐全的营地，那就选择一个离这些设施最远的地方呆着吧。这样，可以确保每天要步行一段距离。选择需要爬坡的线路，在最大程度上进行有氧运动。如果可以，选择那些需要步行而不是开车进入的营地。这样，你每天搭帐篷时，就要到车上去取好几次东西了。

露营对人的心理健康也有好处。我们很多人都生活在压力当中，日程安排得满满的，塞车成为家常便饭，电话铃声响个不断。而欣赏大自然的美景，倾听大自然的声音，会让人的心灵得到宽慰，元气得到恢复。坐在绿色的丛林里，看着一群鸟儿飞过，会让大脑重新回到平静、健康的状态。听着小溪潺潺流淌，可以让你进入深度睡眠，清爽安神。坐在营火旁，感觉皮肤的温暖，工作中的烦恼会烟消云散。

露营使你从日常生活中摆脱出来，让你彻底放松。

我们都知道，一个人感觉越好，气色就越好。露营对身心健康都有好处，让你看起来更加美丽。当你身体变得更加健康、精神变得更加轻松时，就会在身上显现出来。露营可以让你光芒四射，与众不同。

说到光芒四射，别忘了带上足够的照明设备，以便于你在野外过夜。作为设备的一部分，务必带上各种各样的灯具。一个好的手电筒是必不可少的。头灯是非常重要的，以便于在黑暗中需要双手同时在袋子里找东西。如果要坐在野餐桌旁玩扑克牌，一个电池动力荧光灯正好派上用场。如果你打算度一个长假，或者在一个十分偏远的地方露营，那么，最好考虑购买一个由手动曲柄供电的灯具。这样，在电池耗尽后，还可以有一个光源，的确令人欣慰。

通过适当的准备和提前计划，露营在改善你的身心健康方面可以发挥重要作用。所以，走出去，去露营吧，只是晚上睡觉前别忘了关灯。

Section Ⅲ: Passage

Resorts (Part One)

A resort is a place used for relaxation or recreation, attracting visitors for vacations and/or tourism. Resorts are places, towns or sometimes commercial establishment operated by a single company.

In North American English, the term "resort" is now also used for a self-contained commercial establishment which attempts to provide for most of a vacationer's wants while remaining on the premises, such as food, drink, lodging, sports, entertainment, and shopping. The term may be used to identify a hotel property that provides an array of amenities and typically includes entertainment and recreational activities. A hotel is frequently a central feature of a resort, such as the Grand Hotel at Mackinac Island, Michigan. A resort is not always a commercial establishment operated by a single company, although in the late twentieth century this sort of facility became more common.

Resorts fall into different categories.

Towns which are resorts — or where tourism or vacationing is a major part of the local activity — are sometimes called resort towns. If they are by the sea they are called seaside resorts. Inland resorts include ski resorts, mountain resorts and spa towns etc.

An island resort is an island or an archipelago that contains resorts, hotels, restaurants, tourist attractions and its amenities.

Seaside resorts are located on a coast. In the United Kingdom, many seaside towns have turned to other entertainment industries, and some of them have a good deal of nightlife. The cinemas and theatres often remain to become host to a number of pubs, bars, restaurants and nightclubs. Most of their entertainment facilities cater to local people and the beaches still remain popular during the summer months. Although international tourism turned people away from British seaside towns, it also brought in foreign travel and as a result, many seaside towns offer foreign language schools, the students of which often return to vacation and sometimes to settle.

In Europe and North America, ski resorts are towns and villages in ski areas, with support services for skiing such as hotels and chalets, equipment rental, ski schools and ski lifts to access the slopes.

A destination resort is a resort that contains, in and of itself, the necessary guest attraction capabilities. That is to say, a destination resort does not need to be near a destination (town, historic site, theme park, or other) to attract its public. A commercial establishment at a resort destination such as a recreational area, a scenic or historic site, a theme park, a gaming facility or other tourist attraction may compete with other businesses at a destination.

Consequently, another quality of a destination resort is that it offers food, drink, lodging, sports and entertainment, and shopping within the facility so that guests have no need to leave the facility throughout their stay. Commonly these facilities are of higher quality than would be expected if one were to stay at a hotel or eat in a town's restaurants. Closely related to these resorts are convention sites. Generally these occur in cities where special meeting halls, together with ample accommodations as well as varied dining and entertainment, are provided.

课文 2　Text B

Section Ⅰ: Dialog
Interpret the following dialog alternatively into English and Chinese.

客人: Hello.
服务员: 前台, 您好。能为您效劳吗?
客人: Yes, I am checking out.

服务员：谢谢您通知我们。我们马上准备您的账单。
客人：I'll be down in 15 minutes. Please send someone to my room.
服务员：我们马上派人过去。
客人：Thanks.
服务员：您今天早上用过店内的任何服务设施吗？
客人：No, I haven't used any services.
服务员：一切都井然有序。好了，先生，您可以去前台了，她们等着为您结账呢。
客人：Thank you.
服务员：不客气。
客人：Hello. I just called. I'm here to check out.
服务员：您好！这是您的账单。5个晚上，每晚68美元，一共340美元。
客人：Are credit cards accepted here?
服务员：可以。请把您的卡给我。
客人：Sure. Here you are.
服务员：对不起，这张卡不能用。您还有别的卡吗？
客人：Yes, I do. Try this one.
服务员：对不起，也不好用。
客人：That's weird. Does it say why?
服务员：没说什么。就是不好用。
客人：Never mind. I'll pay by cash. Here's 350 dollars.
服务员：谢谢，先生。这是找您的零头。
客人：Thank you.
服务员：好，行了。希望很快能再次为您服务。再见。
客人：Bye.

Section Ⅱ：Passage

Interpret the following passage into Chinese.

Why Travel?

Some people often ask us, "Why do we have to travel?" Let's listen to what Mark Twain said many years ago.

"Twenty years from now you will be more disappointed by the things you didn't do than by the ones you did do. So throw off the bowlines, sail away from the safe harbor. Catch the trade winds in your sails. Explore. Dream. Discover."

The following are 9 reasons why you must travel.

1. You will grow as a person

When you travel the world, you have the opportunity to experience different cultures and meet new people. It is inevitable that through these experiences you will learn a lot about yourself, who you are as a person and what you want out of life.

2. Freedom

You will enjoy a much greater sense of freedom when no one is able to tell you what to do. You are the boss. You decide where you want to go, what you want to do and how long you want to stay.

3. Simplicity

You will discover how much better life can be when you live it simply. No phone, email, TV, job, schedule, bills to pay; just you, your surroundings and your mind. Perfection.

4. Glorious Food

You will have the chance to taste food from all corners of the globe. Do you like eating Chinese, Thai or Indian food? You will enjoy the food even more when you eat it from the place it originated.

5. Meet New People

You will have the chance to meet new people when you travel; some interesting, some boring, and some downright crazy. Everyone has a story to tell, chances are that it will be worth listening to.

6. Nature

Instead of looking out your office window to see a hundred skyscrapers staring back at you, you will get the chance to see the world in all its natural beauty. See the deserts of Africa or the jungles of the Amazon with your own eyes instead of looking at a still image in a book.

7. Become Street Smart

You might already be book smart but add street smart to your persona then there's no stopping you; it's a killer combination. Travelling teaches you many of life's lessons and you will gain pearls of wisdom along your journey; from being able to barter, to knowing when you are trying to be conned, there are many things new places can teach you.

8. You only live once

We all get a limited amount of time on this Earth, and no one knows when it will come to an end (sorry, to be such a downer). Do you really want to stay in the same town or city your whole life, without meeting new people, tasting new foods and seeing and experiencing life as others do?

9. Coming Home

After travelling round the world, there is nothing quite like the feeling of walking through your front door, dropping your bags on the floor, and going upstairs to sleep in your warm, comfortable bed for a day or two. As much fun as travelling can be, everyone needs a place they can call home.

Section Ⅲ: Passage
Interpret the following passage into English.

度假胜地（第二部分）

套餐式度假村收取固定的费用，提供大多数项目或所有项目。套餐式度假村至少包括住宿、餐饮、体育活动和娱乐活动，价格固定。

一些套餐式度假村专为特殊人群设计。例如，某些度假村只接纳成人游客，有的更专业，只接纳夫妻、情侣。其他套餐式度假村则面向家庭，有手工艺中心、游戏室和水上公园，让所有年龄段的儿童都能够乐在其中。套餐式度假村也是备受青睐的婚礼举办地。

温泉度假村是一个短期的住宿设施，主要目的是为喜欢泡温泉的人提供个性化服务，使其养成良好的健康习惯。从历史上看，上述地方大都是在天然温泉或矿泉水源头所在地开发的。一般7天为1个周期，提供全面服务，包括水疗服务、健身活动、健康教育、健康美食和特殊兴趣培养等。

高尔夫度假村，顾名思义，就是专门为热爱高尔夫运动的人准备的，包括有权使用一个或多个高尔夫球场或俱乐部。高尔夫度假村通常提供套餐服务，包括高尔夫球场、球车、练习球、住宿、饮食等。

在北美，滑雪胜地一般是指滑雪区里的综合旅游度假区，不太可能指城镇或村庄。

度假胜地可以是一个高档度假区，通常包括很多活动、很多景点，如高尔夫、水上运动、水疗美容设施、滑雪、自然生态与享受宁静等。鉴于其提供设施的范围，可以将其视为综合旅游度假区。

大型度假村是一种综合旅游度假区，规模很大，如拉斯维加斯大道两旁的度假胜地。在新加坡，综合旅游度假区是包括赌场在内的度假区的委婉表达方式。

度假村在欧洲指的是设施齐全、自给自足的度假胜地，住宿的地方通常是别墅。在英国，度假营地指的是一个度假胜地，住宿的地方通常是木造农舍。"假日公园"这一术语通常是指度假胜地的住宿包括由汽车拖行的临时度假屋和木造农舍。

参考答案

Section Ⅰ: Dialog

客人：您好。

服务员：Hi, front desk. Can I help you?

客人：嗯，我准备结账。

服务员：Thanks for calling. We'll prepare your bill right away.

客人：我一刻钟后下去。请派人到我房间检查一下。

服务员：We'll be right there.

客人：谢谢。

服务员：Have you used any hotel services this morning?

客人：没有，没用过。

服务员：Everything is in perfect order. OK, sir, you can go to the front desk now. They are ready to check you out.

客人：谢谢。

服务员：Anytime.

客人：您好。我刚打过电话。我要结账。

服务员：Hello. Here's your bill. Five nights at 68 dollars each. That makes a total of 340 dollars.

客人：可以刷卡吗？

服务员：Yes. May I have your card, please?

客人：好的，给。

服务员：Sorry, this card doesn't go through. Do you have another one?

客人：有，试试这张。

服务员：Sorry, it doesn't work, either.

客人：这就怪了。系统上怎么说的？

服务员：No. It just doesn't work.

客人：没事，我用现金支付。这是 350 美元。

服务员：Thank you, sir. And here's your change.

客人：谢谢。

服务员：OK, that's it. We are looking forward to hosting you again soon. Goodbye.

客人：再见。

Section Ⅱ：Passage

旅游的理由

有人经常问我们："为什么一定要去旅游？"让我们听听马克·吐温许多年前是怎么说的吧。

"20年以后，你可能会为自己所做过的事情感到后悔，但你更会为所没做过的事情感到后悔。那么，请解开系紧的船缆，驶离安全的港湾，扬帆远航吧！去探索！去追梦！去发现吧！"

下面是我们必须旅游的9大理由。

一、变得成熟

周游世界让你有机会领略不同的文化，结交新的朋友。通过这些经历，你会自然而然地加深对自己的了解，你会更加清楚自己究竟是个什么样的人，更加清楚自己对生活的期望是什么。

二、享受自由

没有人能告诉该做什么，你将享受更大的自由。一切你自己说了算。去哪儿、做什么、待多久，都由你自己决定。

三、返璞归真

你会发现，简朴的生活才是更好的生活。没有电话、没有电子邮件、没有电视、没有工作、没有时间表、没有账单要付，有的只是你自己、你周边的环境和你的心灵。多么完美！

四、美酒佳肴

你将有机会品尝世界各个角落的食物。你喜欢吃中国菜、泰国菜，还是印度菜？当你在这些美食的家乡就餐时，一定会感到别有风味。

五、结交新朋

旅行中有机会结识新朋友，有的风趣，有的沉闷，有的简直不可理喻。每个人都有自己的故事，而有些故事也许真的值得一听。

六、亲近自然

你将有机会亲眼目睹这个世界的自然美丽，而不必透过办公室的窗户与上百座摩天大楼相视无语。亲眼看看非洲的沙漠或者亚马逊丛林，那可绝对不是书本上呆板的图片能比得上的。

七、学乖学精

你可能很会读书，但要是再有一些生存能力，你将所向披靡，战无不胜，因为这种结合是再完美不过了。旅行会教给你生活中的许多经验教训，你一边旅行，一边采撷智慧的珍珠。从讨价还价到不受蒙骗，每到一个地方，都会有新的收获。

八、人生有涯

我们每个人在这个地球上的时间都是有限的，没有人知道大限何时到来（不好意思，这样说，有点令人感到不快）。你真的想一辈子都待在同一个地方吗？真的不想像他人那样去结识新朋友、品尝新食物、见见大世面、体验新生活吗？

九、回家真好

周游世界后，还有什么能比回家更惬意的事情？穿过前门，顺手将行李扔在地板上，走上楼去，一头扎进温暖舒适的床上，睡上一两天。尽管旅游充满乐趣，但每个人都需要一个他们称之为家的地方。

Section Ⅲ: Passage

Resorts (Part Two)

An all-inclusive resort charges a fixed price that includes most or all items. At a minimum, most inclusive resorts include lodging, unlimited food, drink, sports activities, and entertainment for the fixed price.

Some all-inclusive resorts are designed for specific vacation interests. For example, certain resorts cater to adults, while even more specialized properties accept couples only. Other all-inclusive resorts are geared toward families, with facilities like craft centers, game rooms and water parks to keep children of all ages entertained. All inclusive resorts are also very popular locations for destination weddings.

A spa resort is a short term residential/lodging facility with the primary purpose of providing individual services for spa-goers to develop healthy habits. Historically many such spas were developed at the location of natural hot springs or sources of mineral waters. Typically over a seven-day stay, such facilities provide a comprehensive program that includes spa services, physical fitness activities, wellness education, healthy cuisine and special interest programming.

Golf resorts are, as its name suggests, resorts that cater specifically to the sport of golf, and include access to one or more golf course and or clubhouse. Golf resorts typically provide golf packages that provide visitors with all greens and cart fees, range balls, accommodations and meals.

In North America a ski resort is generally a destination resort in a ski area, and is less likely to refer to a town or village.

A resort can be an expensive vacation and often boasts many visitor activities and attractions such as golf, water sports, spa and beauty facilities, skiing, natural ecology and tranquility. Because of the extent of amenities offered, it may be considered a destination resort.

A megaresort is a type of destination resort which is of an exceptionally large size, such as those along the Las Vegas Strip. In Singapore an integrated resort is a euphemism for a casino-based destination resort.

A holiday village is a type of self-contained resort in Europe, where the accommodation is generally in villas. A holiday camp in the United Kingdom refers to a resort where the accommodation is in chalets. The term "holiday park" is used for a resort where the accommodation includes caravans and chalets.

第3单元
问路指点

Asking for Directions

课文 1　Text A

Section Ⅰ：Dialog
Interpret the following dialog alternatively into English and Chinese.

游客：Excuse me, sir, I want to go to the International Horticultural Exhibition.

路人：嗯，您算问对人了。沿着这条路往前走，在第二个路口往左拐。汽车站就在附近。

游客：By the way, which bus shall I take?

路人：噢，我差点忘了。110路。

游客：Do I have to change buses?

路人：不用，这是世园会专线车。

游客：A shuttle bus? How do I pay?

路人：上车付钱。这是无人售票车。

游客：You mean I put my money right in the machine?

路人：对，把钱投入投币口。

游客：How much does it cost?

路人：12元。您知道，世园会在郊区，离市中心很远。

游客：I see.

路人：通常需要准备好零钱，巴士上不找零。

游客：I know. Well, how many stops are there?

路人：一共20站。

游客：Oh, that's far. And then I get off at the terminal?

路人：对。下车后，您会看到一个巨大的指示牌，上面写着"世界园艺博览会"。您不会错过的。

游客：Well, how often does the shuttle bus run?

路人：20分钟一趟。

游客：Speaking of time, I think I'd better hurry up. Sorry for taking up so much of your precious time.

路人：没什么。很高兴能帮上您的忙。祝您好运。再见。

游客：Bye.

Section Ⅱ: Passage
Interpret the following passage into Chinese.

The Grand Canyon

The Grand Canyon is a steep-sided canyon carved by the Colorado River in the United States in the state of Arizona. It is 446 kilometers long, up to 29 kilometers wide and attains a depth of over 1,800 meters. For thousands of years, the area has been continuously inhabited by Native Americans who built settlements within the canyon and its many caves. The first European known to have viewed the Grand Canyon was a Spanish explorer, who arrived in 1540.

Although the Grand Canyon is not the deepest canyon in the world, it is known for its visually overwhelming size and its intricate and colorful landscape. Geologically it is significant because of the thick sequence of ancient rocks that are beautifully preserved and exposed in the walls of the canyon. These rock layers record much of the early geologic history of the North American continent.

The Grand Canyon is part of the Colorado River basin which has developed over the past 40 million years. A recent study places the origins of the canyon beginning about 17 million years ago. Previous estimates had placed the age of the canyon at 5-6 million years. The canyon is the result of erosion which creates one of the most complete geologic columns on the planet.

Weather in the Grand Canyon varies according to elevation. The forested rims are high enough to receive winter snowfall, but along the Colorado River in the Inner Gorge, temperatures are similar to those found in Tucson and other low elevation desert locations in Arizona.

There are approximately 1,737 known species of vascular plants, 167 species of fungi, 64 species of moss and 195 species of lichen found in Grand Canyon National Park. This variety is largely due to the 8,000-foot elevation change from the Colorado River up to the highest point on the North Rim. The Grand Canyon boasts a dozen endemic plants while only 10% of the Park's flora is exotic. Sixty-three plants found here have been given special status by the U.S. Fish and Wildlife Service. Besides, there are 34 mammal species found along the Colorado River corridor, of which 18 are rodents and eight are bats.

The Grand Canyon area has some of the cleanest air in the United States. However, at times the air quality can be considerably affected by events such as forest fires and dust storms in the Southwest.

Section Ⅲ: Passage
Interpret the following passage into English.

夏季旅行

　　夏天到了，生活很惬意。对许多美国人来说，这是一个旅行的季节。为什么？因为学校放假了，因为天气很好，最为重要的是，我们都应该给自己放个假了。美国人休假时，常常去他们心仪的度假胜地。

　　纵观历史，美国人一直是一个迁徙中的民族。早期移民经过长途跋涉来到新大陆。他们刚一登陆，就在东海岸定居。然而，他们并不满足于长期待在那里。探险家和商人前往西部未知领域。之后，移民也向西迁移，开发这些新的地区。由于西进运动，美国人最后占据了从大西洋到太平洋的整块新大陆。即便是在今天，美国人似乎仍然无法在一地久留。研究表明，美国人平均5年要搬1次家。

　　除了喜欢搬家以外，美国人也很喜欢旅行。一些人每天上下班都要赶不少路，甚至需要经常出差。大部分公司会给员工放年假，人们通常会利用这段时间去旅行。有些人会去远一点的州走亲访友，有些人则在周末去一趟花费少的短途旅行，住在花费不高的汽车旅馆里。品味较高的人选择豪华的度假胜地和高级饭店，酷爱探险的人则会前往绝佳的户外营地。有些人开着房车出游，舒舒服服地体验露营生活，有些人则睡在帐篷里，尝试纯粹的野外生活。

　　大多数美国人喜欢在国内旅游。为什么？其中一个原因是，国内旅游比国外旅游便宜，而且，也没有语言不通的问题。此外，美国幅员辽阔，有众多的旅游景点。爱好大自然的人可以去海滩、大山、峡谷、湖泊等地旅游，欣赏许许多多的自然奇观。大城市也给游客提供了都市特有的乐趣。如今，有了现代高速公路、铁路和飞机，在美国旅行变得易如反掌。

　　美国的很多度假项目非常特别，和选择这些项目的人一样特别。全家出游时，通常会优先考虑孩子。越来越多适合"全家游"的度假胜地为孩子提供特别的活动。对历史感兴趣的人会参观历史名胜和博物馆。环保人士则喜欢"绿色旅游"，这样的旅行使他们能近距离观察动植物，并且不会扰乱大自然敏感的生态平衡。有些人觉得海上航游使人心情放松，神清气爽，有些人则到水边垂钓、滑水或激流漂流。勇敢的人会到亚洲和非洲去徒步探险、去游猎，享受一辈子难得一次的刺激。

　　美国人不是世上唯一喜爱旅行的。跨国企业、大众传播与喷气式飞机的出现让很多人成为环球旅游者。世界各地的人们都喜欢到海外旅游。不管哪国人，也都喜欢到自己国内的景区去看看。不过，忙忙碌碌、四处奔走造就了美国人的个性，那就是不断在迁徙。几乎每个美国人都有旅行的经历。

参考答案

Section I：Dialog

游客：先生，劳驾，请问去世界园艺博览会怎么走？

路人：Well, you are talking to the right guy here. Down this road, and take the second turning on the left. And you will see a bus stop nearby.

游客：对了，坐几路车？

路人：Oh, I nearly forgot. Bus No. 110.

游客：要转车吗？

路人：No, you don't have to. It's a shuttle bus to the Exhibition.

游客：专线车？ 怎么付钱？

路人：Pay when you get on. This is a pay-to-the-driver bus.

游客：您的意思是，我把钱投进机器里？

路人：Yes, put your money in the slot.

游客：车票多少钱？

路人：It costs 12 *yuan*. You know, the Exhibition is in the suburbs, far away from downtown.

游客：明白了。

路人：Usually exact fare is required because you can't get change back on a bus.

游客：知道了。嗯，共有多少站？

路人：There are 20 stops.

游客：噢，不近啊。然后，我在终点站下车？

路人：Yes. After that, you will see a huge sign, which says International Horticultural Exhibition. You won't miss it.

游客：嗯，多长时间一趟？

路人：Every 20 minutes.

游客：说到时间，我想我得赶快走了。不好意思，耽误您这么多宝贵时间。

路人：It's all right. I'm glad I could help you out. Good luck. Have a good one.

游客：再见。

Section Ⅱ: Passage

科罗拉多大峡谷

科罗拉多大峡谷是由科罗拉多河侵蚀而成的陡峭峡谷。它位于美国亚利桑那州，长446千米，最宽处达29千米，深1800多米。几千年来，这一地区一直居住着美国土著，他们在峡谷内及洞穴中建造定居点。第一个来到大峡谷的欧洲人是一位西班牙探险家，他是在1540年到达的。

虽然科罗拉多大峡谷不是世界上最深的峡谷，但是，它却以其冲击视觉的大小、错综复杂的地形、丰富多彩的景观而闻名于世。其地质意义十分重大，因为那暴露在峡谷峭壁上的古老岩层均保存完好。这些岩层记录了早期北美大陆的地质史。

科罗拉多大峡谷是科罗拉多河流域的一部分，该流域是在过去4000万年里逐步形成的。最近的一项研究表明，科罗拉多大峡谷起源于1700万年前左右。过去，人们认为大峡谷的年龄五六百万年。科罗拉多大峡谷是河流侵蚀的结果，形成了地球上最完整的地质柱状剖面之一。

科罗拉多大峡谷的天气因海拔的不同而不同。那些长满森林的边缘地区，因为地势很高，能够承受冬季的降雪。但是，在沿着科罗拉多河的谷底深处，温度与亚利桑那州图森市和其他低海拔沙漠地区类似。

在科罗拉多大峡谷国家公园，已知的维管植物大约有1737种，菌类167种，苔藓64种，地衣195种。此处植物的多样性在很大程度上是其由海拔决定的，从科罗拉多河到最高的北缘海拔相差8000英尺。大峡谷有十几种特有的植物，公园内只有10%的植物是外来的。这里有63种植物被美国鱼类和野生生物局赋予了特殊地位。除此之外，在科罗拉多河走廊还发现了34种哺乳动物，其中18种为啮齿动物，8种为蝙蝠。

科罗拉多大峡谷地区有着美国最干净的空气。然而，有时候，森林大火和西南地区的沙尘暴等也会严重影响空气的质量。

Section Ⅲ: Passage

Summer and Travel

It's summertime, and the living is easy. For many Americans, this is the season to travel. Why? Because school is out. Because the weather is great. And most of all, because we all deserve a break. When Americans take a break, they often head for their favorite vacation spot.

Throughout their history, Americans have been people on the move. The early immigrants had to travel to get to the New World. Once they arrived, they settled along the East Coast. But they weren't content to stay there. Explorers and traders journeyed to the unknown western territories. Later, settlers moved west to develop these new areas. As a result of this westward migration, Americans eventually occupied the whole continent-from the Atlantic to the Pacific. Even today, Americans seem unable to stay put. Research says that the average American moves every five years.

Besides their habit of changing addresses, Americans are used to traveling. Some people make long-distance commutes to work daily. Their jobs may even require them to take frequent business trips. Most companies provide an annual vacation for their employees, and people often use that time to travel. Some people just visit friends or relatives in distant states. Others go on low-budget weekend excursions and stay in economy motels. Those with more expensive tastes choose luxurious resorts and hotels. Camping out in the great outdoors appeals to adventurous types. Some travel in recreational vehicles to camp out in comfort, while others "rough it" by sleeping in tents.

Most Americans prefer to travel within their nation's borders. Why? For one thing, it's cheaper than traveling abroad. And there's no language problem. But besides that, the vast American territory offers numerous tourist attractions. Nature lovers can enjoy beaches, mountains, canyons, lakes and a wealth of natural wonders. Major cities offer visitors a multitude of urban delights. The convenience of modern freeways, railways and airplanes makes travel in America as easy as pie.

Many American vacations are as unique as the people who take them. Families often plan their trips with the kids in mind. More and more "family friendly" vacation resorts offer special programs for children. History buffs seek out famous historical sites and museums. Environmentalists prefer "green vacations". These trips allow them to observe flora and fauna up-close without disturbing the sensitive balance of nature. Some people find sea cruises relaxing and refreshing. Others hit the water to go fishing, skiing or white-water rafting. Daring souls get the thrill of a lifetime on trekking expeditions and safaris in remote places from Africa to Asia.

Americans aren't the only people in the world who travel. International business, mass communication and jet airplanes have created a world of globetrotters. People all over the world enjoy going abroad to travel. And no matter where they live, people also enjoy visiting scenic spots in their own country. But being on the go makes Americans what they are: people on the move. In America, almost everybody is a tourist sometimes.

课文 2　Text B

Section Ⅰ: Dialog
Interpret the following dialog alternatively into English and Chinese.

游客: Excuse me, Miss. I'm a stranger here. Can you tell me how to get to the Huangdao District Government?

路人: 外地人? 可我听不出您是哪儿的口音。您是哪里人?

游客: Wuhan.

路人: 哦。您要去黄岛区政府? 有很多走法。

游客: Yes?

路人: 您可以坐渡轮去,也可以坐公交车去,您还可以走跨海大桥或者海底隧道。

游客: I have never traveled by ferry. Maybe I should give it a shot today.

路人: 今天我想是不行了,现在雾多大啊。

游客: You are right. Well…

路人: 嗯,不赶时间的话,可以走环胶州湾高速公路。当然,这个时间要长一点。

游客: How about the Bay Bridge?

路人: 这个快些。这是肯定的了。此外,您可以领略世界上最长的跨海大桥的风采。我觉得这是一次很好的经历。如果您愿意,还可以拍一些不错的照片呢。

游客: Sounds like a good idea. Hold on. You also mentioned the Submarine Tunnel. What's that? I've never heard of that.

路人: 嗯,它是我国最长、世界第三的海底隧道。最深处在海面下82.81米。

游客: Wow, that's amazing. I think I'm going to use the tunnel. But how can I get to the entrance of the tunnel?

路人: 您看见前方的车站了吧?

游客: Yes.

路人: 坐321路公交车,在团岛站下车,然后换乘隧道3线。

游客: Bus No. 321, then the Tuandao Stop, and then Tunnel Line 3.

路人: 对。在区政府站下车,在您的右边,可以看到几栋办公楼。

游客: Thanks. I really appreciate your help.

路人：不客气。祝您度过美好的一天。

游客：You too.

Section Ⅱ: Passage
Interpret the following passage into Chinese.

The London Eye

The London Eye is a giant Ferris wheel on the south bank of the River Thames in London. Also known as the Millennium Wheel, its official name was originally the British Airways London Eye, then the Merlin Entertainments London Eye, and since January 2011, the EDF Energy London Eye.

The entire structure is 135 meters tall and the wheel has a diameter of 120 meters. It is currently Europe's tallest Ferris wheel, and the most popular paid tourist attraction in the United Kingdom with over 3.5 million visitors annually, and it has made many appearances in popular culture.

When erected in 1999 it was the world's tallest Ferris wheel, until it was surpassed first by the 160-meter Star of Nanchang in 2006 followed by the 165-meter Singapore Flyer in 2008 and lastly the 167.6-meter High Roller in 2014. Supported by an A-frame on one side only, unlike the taller Nanchang and Singapore wheels, the Eye is described by its operators as "the world's tallest cantilevered observation wheel". It offered the highest public viewing point in the city until it was superseded by the 245-meter observation deck on the 72nd floor of The Shard, which opened to the public on February 1, 2013.

The London Eye adjoins the western end of Jubilee Gardens on the South Bank of the River Thames between Westminster Bridge and Hungerford Bridge, in the London Borough of Lambeth.

The London Eye was formally opened by the then Prime Minister Tony Blair on December 31, 1999, although it was not opened to the public until March 9, 2000 because of technical problems. On June 5, 2008 it was announced that 30 million people had ridden the London Eye since it opened.

The wheel's 32 sealed and air-conditioned ovoidal passenger capsules are attached to the external circumference of the wheel and rotated by electric motors. Each of the 10-tonne capsules represents one of the London Boroughs, and holds up to 25 people, who are free to walk around inside the capsule, though seating is provided.

The Eye exists in a category of its own. It essentially has to fulfill only one function, and what a brilliantly inessential function it is: to lift people up from the ground, take them round a giant loop in the sky, then put them back down where they started. That is all it needs to do, and thankfully, that is all it does.

The Eye has done for London what the Eiffel Tower did for Paris, which is to give it a symbol and to let people climb above the city and look back down on it. Not just specialists or rich people, but everybody. That's the beauty of it: it is public and accessible, and it is in a great position at the heart of London.

Section Ⅲ: Passage
Interpret the following passage into English.

泰　山

泰山，世界文化与自然双重遗产，是一座历史文化名山。泰山位于我国山东省泰安市北面，最高峰玉皇顶海拔1545米。

泰山是五岳之一。说到泰山，人们就会把它跟日出、新生和再生联系在一起，被视为五岳之首。

在旧石器时代，这里便出现了人类的踪迹。在新石器时代，人类便在这里定居，这一点已经得到证实。在此期间，泰山附近出现了两种文化，即南部的大汶口文化和北部的龙山文化。

这里树林茂密，植被覆盖面积达到79.9%。这里的植物多种多样，已知的物种达到989种，其中433种为树木，其余的为草本植物。药用植物共计462种，其中包括何首乌、泰山参、紫草和黄精，享誉全国。有些树非常古老，非常有名，尤其是汉代柏树、迎客松和五大夫松。此外，除122种鸟类，还有其他200多种动物。

据史料记载，在公元前1000多年的周朝，泰山便已成为历代帝王所钟情的献祭和打坐的圣地，先后有72位皇帝来此拜谒。文人墨客也纷纷前来，获取灵感，舞文弄诗，画画拍照。因此，山上留下了大量文物。

游客要想到达山顶，可以先坐车到中天门，然后乘索道登顶。步行则需要2.5~6小时。小商小贩沿途叫卖的货物都是由脚夫从中天门或者泰山脚下背上去的。

爬山有两条线。颇受欢迎的东线从泰山拱门开始，一路共有7200个石阶，登山者先要经过万仙楼、罗汉崖和斗母宫。从一天门出发，手脚麻利的游客需要2.5小时，对于安步当车的游客来说，则需要6小时。从一天门到中天门，快走需要1

小时，漫步则需要2.5小时。在斗母宫的东北是经石峪，上刻佛教典籍《金刚经》，字径50厘米，据信为北魏时期雕刻作品。西线走的人相对不多，风景更多，但文化遗产较少。

Section Ⅰ：Dialog

游客：小姐，打扰了。我是外地人。请问去黄岛区政府怎么走？

路人：A stranger? But I can't find out your accent. Where are you from?

游客：武汉人。

路人：I see. So you want the Huangdao District Government? There are many ways to get there.

游客：是吗？

路人：You can get there by ferry or by bus. You can also use the Bay Bridge, or the Submarine Tunnel.

游客：我从没坐过渡轮，也许今天该试一试。

路人：I don't think you can do it this time, as it is very foggy now.

游客：您说得对。嗯……

路人：Well, if you are not in a hurry, you may use the Expressway along the Jiaozhou Bay, which, of course, takes a longer time.

游客：那跨海大桥呢？

路人：It's faster. That's for sure. Besides, you can enjoy the longest sea bridge in the world. I think it's a good experience. And you can take some wonderful photos if you are in the mood.

游客：好主意。等一下。您刚才还提到了海底隧道。那是什么？我从没听说过。

路人：Oh, it is the longest undersea tunnel in China and the third longest in the world. It is 82.81 meters below the sea level at its deepest section.

游客：噢，太了不起了！我要走隧道。可是，怎样才能到达隧道入口呢？

路人：You see the bus stop up ahead?

游客：看见了。

路人：Take Bus No. 321, get off at the Tuandao Stop, and change to Tunnel Line 3.

游客：321路公交车，团岛站，然后是隧道3线。

路人：Yes. Get off at the District Government stop, and you can see some office buildings on your right.

游客：谢谢。多谢您的帮助。
路人：My pleasure. Have a nice day.
游客：您也一样。

Section II: Passage

伦 敦 眼

　　伦敦眼是坐落在伦敦泰晤士河南岸的一个巨大的摩天轮。伦敦眼也叫千禧轮，其正式名称最初是英航伦敦眼，接着是梅林娱乐伦敦眼，从 2011 年 1 月开始，又叫作英国电网伦敦眼。

　　伦敦眼高 135 米，直径 120 米。目前，它是欧洲最高的摩天轮，也是英国最受欢迎的付费旅游景点，每年接待 350 多万游客，因此，常常在流行文化中一展风采。

　　1999 年建成时，伦敦眼是世界上最高的摩天轮，后来被在 2006 年建的高 160 米的南昌之星超过，再后来先后被 2008 年建成的高 165 米的新加坡摩天观景轮和 2014 年建成的高 167.6 米的疯狂转轮超过。与南昌之星和新加坡摩天观景轮不同，伦敦眼只是在一侧由一个 A 字型架构支撑着，被其运营商描述为"世界上最高的悬臂式观景摩天轮"。这是当时伦敦最高的公共观景处，后来，被位于碎片大厦 72 层、高 245 米的观景台取代，该观景台于 2013 年 2 月 1 日向公众开放。

　　伦敦眼毗连泰晤士河南岸的银禧花园西端，介于伦敦兰贝斯区威斯敏斯特桥和亨格福德桥之间。

　　伦敦眼是由时任英国首相的托尼·布莱尔于 1999 年 12 月 31 日正式揭幕的。不过，由于技术问题，直到 2000 年 3 月 9 日才向公众开放。2008 年 6 月 5 日，对外宣布，自开业以来，乘坐伦敦眼的人数已经达到了 3000 万。

　　摩天轮有 32 个带空调的密封卵形乘客舱，连接到其外周缘，由电动机提供旋转动力。每个乘客舱重 10 吨，分别代表伦敦的一个区，能容纳 25 人。乘客可以在舱内自由走动，当然，也可以坐在座位上。

　　伦敦眼以其独特的风格自成一家。从本质上说，它只需要满足一个功能即可。那个十分突出却又无关紧要的功能，就是让人离开地面，带着他们在天空中转一个大圈，然后，把他们送回到原来的地方。这就是它所需要做的全部内容。值得庆幸的是，事实上，它也是这么做的。

　　伦敦眼之于伦敦，正如埃菲尔铁塔之于巴黎。它是伦敦的一个象征，让人爬到城市上空，俯瞰城市。它不仅属于专家、富人，也属于每一个人。这就是它的美妙之所在。它是大家的，是每个人都可以乘坐的。而且，它处在伦敦市中心一个极佳的位置上。

Section Ⅲ: Passage

Mount Tai

Mount Tai, a world cultural heritage site as well as a world natural heritage site, is a mountain of historical and cultural significance located north of the city of Tai'an, in Shandong Province, China. The tallest peak, the Jade Emperor Peak, is 1,545 meters tall.

Mount Tai is one of the Five Great Mountains. It is associated with sunrise, birth, and renewal, and is regarded as the foremost of the five.

Traces of human presence at Mount Tai date back to the Paleolithic period. Human settlement of the area can be proven from the Neolithic period onwards. During this time, two cultures had emerged near the mountain, the Dawenkou culture to the south and the Longshan culture to the north.

Vegetation covers 79.9% of the area, which is densely wooded. The flora is diverse and known to comprise 989 species, of which 433 species are woody and the rest herbaceous. Medicinal plants total 462 species, including multi-flower knotweed, Taishan ginseng, Chinese gromwell and sealwort, which are renowned throughout the country. Some trees are very old and famous, notably the Han Dynasty Cypresses, Welcoming Guest Pine and Fifth Rank Pine. And here are over 200 species of animals in addition to 122 species of birds.

According to historical records, Mount Tai became a sacred place haunted by emperors to offer sacrifices and meditate in the Zhou Dynasty before 1,000 BC. A total of 72 emperors were recorded as visiting it. Men of letters also came to acquire inspiration, compose poems, write essays, paint and take pictures. Hence, a great many cultural relics were left on the mountain.

Visitors can reach the peak of Mount Tai via a bus which terminates at the Midway Gate to Heaven, from there a cable car connects to the summit. Covering the same distance on foot takes from two and a half to six hours. The supplies for the many vendors along the road to the summit are carried up by porters either from the Midway Gate to Heaven or all the way up from the foot of the mountain.

To climb up the mountain, one can take one of two routes. The more popular east route starts from Taishan Arch. On the way up the 7,200 stone steps, the climber first passes the Ten Thousand Immortals Tower, Arhat Cliff, and Palace to Goddess Dou Mu. The climbing from the First Gate to Heaven up the entire mountain can take two and a half hours for the sprinting hiker to six hours for the leisure pace. Reaching the Midway Gate to Heaven from First Gate to Heaven is one hour at a sprint up to two and a half hours leisurely. To the northeast of the Palace to Goddess Dou Mu is Sutra Rock Valley in which the Buddhist Diamond Sutra was cut in characters measuring fifty centimeters across believed to be inscribed in the Northern Wei Dynasty. The west route, taken by fewer tourists, is more scenic, but has less cultural heritage.

第4单元

观光游览

Sight-seeing

课文 1　Text A

Section Ⅰ: Dialog

Interpret the following dialog alternatively into English and Chinese.

导游：Hi, Kevin. Is this your first trip to Qingdao?

游客：是的，第一次。

导游：Then welcome to Qingdao.

游客：谢谢。琳达，您知道，我不会在这儿待很长时间。有什么值得一看吗？

导游：The coast. It's a must for tourists, I should say.

游客：海边？我知道青岛三面环海，一面靠山。海边有什么特别的吗？

导游：Certainly. The city's most scenic drive follows a costal route.

游客：是吗？说来听听。

导游：Let's begin with the Pier. It was built in 1891 as a military wharf. Later, when Germany occupied Qingdao in 1897, it was turned into a shipping dock. Today, it has become a symbol of the city. They say that a trip to Qingdao is not complete without a visit to the Pier.

游客：是吗？德国占领？怪不得从飞机上看，青岛就像德国的城市一样。

导游：Really. It is probably the most visited place in Qingdao, where you can see people feeding seagulls if you are lucky enough.

游客：海鸥？真是人与自然的和谐统一啊！

导游：If you take a walk along the coast, you will find many tourist attractions, such as Little Qingdao, on which there is a beacon, the Little Fish Hill, which commands a good view of the city, the Navy Museum, the Underwater World, the First Bathing Beach, one of the 6 bathing beaches in Qingdao and the largest one in Asia, the Olympic Sailing Center, the buildings of various architectural styles, known as the Universal Expo of Architectures, the Polar Aquarium, to name but a few.

游客：听来很不错。我都等不及了。

导游：What is worth special mentioning is the boardwalk along the coast. It is 36.9 kilometers long, running, from the west to the east, through 7 scenic areas.

游客：也就是可以领略当地人所说的"红瓦绿树，碧海蓝天"了。

导游：You can say that again. The parks and gardens, the sun and the beaches provide a peaceful contrast to the city bustle.

游客：可以想象得到。生活在这里的人们真是幸福啊！

导游: Then what are we waiting for? Let's go enjoy the sights along the way.

游客: 好，走。

Section II: Passage
Interpret the following passage into Chinese.

Amsterdam

Amsterdam is the capital city of the Kingdom of the Netherlands. Its status as the Dutch capital is mandated by the Constitution of the Netherlands though it is not the seat of the Dutch government, which is at the Hague.

Amsterdam is located in the western Netherlands, in the Province of North Holland. The river Amstel terminates in the city center and connects to a large number of canals that eventually terminate in the IJ Bay. Amsterdam is situated 2 meters below sea level. The surrounding land is flat as it is formed of large polders. A man made forest is situated southwest. Amsterdam is connected to the North Sea through the long North Sea Canal.

As the commercial and cultural capital of the country and one of the top financial centers in Europe, Amsterdam is considered an alpha world city by the Globalization and World Cities study group. Many large Dutch institutions have their headquarters there, and 7 of the world's top 500 companies are based in the city.

Amsterdam is home to more than one hundred kilometers of canals. In the Middle Ages, Amsterdam was surrounded by a moat, which now forms the innermost ring in the city, and makes the city center a horseshoe shape. The city is also served by a seaport. It is often nicknamed the "Venice of the North", due to its division into approximately 90 islands, which are linked by more than 1,200 bridges.

The Amsterdam canal system is the result of conscious city planning. In the early 17th century, when immigration was at a peak, a comprehensive plan was developed that was based on four concentric half-circles of canals with their ends emerging at the IJ Bay. The canals served for defense, water management and transport.

Amsterdam is one of the most popular tourist destinations in Europe, receiving more than 4.63 million international visitors annually. This excludes the 16 million day trippers visiting the city every year. The number of visitors has been growing steadily over the past decade. This can be attributed to an increasing number of European visitors. Two thirds of the hotels are located in the city's center. Hotels with 4 or 5 stars contribute 42% of the total beds available and 41% of the overnight stays in Amsterdam. The room occupation rate was 78% in 2006, up from 70% in 2005. The majority of tourists (74%) originate from Europe. The largest group of non-European visitors comes from the United States, accounting for 14% of the total. Certain years have a theme in Amsterdam to attract extra tourists. Some hotels offer special arrangements or activities during these years. The average number of guests per year staying at the four campsites around the city ranges from 12,000 to 65,000.

Section Ⅲ: Passage
Interpret the following passage into English.

西双版纳

"西双版纳"又叫 *Sipsongpanna*，是我国南方云南省南部的一个自治州。州政府所在地是景洪，是该区最大的居民点，横跨澜沧江。

Sipsongpanna 是一个傣语合成词。*Sipsong* 的意思是"12"，*panna* 的意思是"1000亩或约67公顷的土地"。"西双版纳"指的是传统上把"勐"，即半独立的城邦或公国，分成了12个行政区。

自治州面积19700平方千米。西双版纳是傣族人民的家园。该地区的海拔高度低于云南大部分地区，属热带气候。它正迅速成为一个受人追捧的旅游目的地。

西双版纳地区蕴藏着云南种类最多的生物，而云南则蕴藏着全国种类最多的生物。究其原因，一是热带气候，二是地处偏远。不过，地处偏远之说近来有所改变。除了各种各样的植物以外，西双版纳还是为数不多的亚洲象在我国的家园。直到几百年前，这些大象还出没在全国的大部分地区。如今，它们生活在保护区内。可是，植物多样性却因橡胶种植园的泛滥而受到威胁。橡胶种植园彻底摧毁了热带雨林，取而代之的是来自巴西的单一树种。

州内的六大茶区生产一些20世纪最受追捧的普洱茶。

西双版纳有着丰富的自然资源、历史资源和文化资源，以其民间传说、雨林及珍稀植物和野生动物而闻名。其主要旅游景点包括曼飞龙佛塔、景真八角亭、野象谷以及橄榄坝镇上的傣族村。特别值得一提的是西双版纳热带植物园。该研究机构成立于1959年，隶属于中国科学院，从事生物多样性保护和植物资源可持续利用的研究。它坐落在西双版纳的勐腊县，占地1125公顷，35个标本园内保存着13000多种热带植物。

著名的传统节日是傣族的泼水节，4 月 13 日开始，15 日结束，先后历时 3 天。此外，还有一些其他活动，如赛龙舟、发射土制导弹、放孔明灯等。

自 1990 年西双版纳嘎洒机场（原"景洪国际机场"）投入使用以来，乘飞机前往西双版纳变得越来越普遍，越来越方便。每天都有航班穿梭于西双版纳和昆明之间。该地区也有飞往大理、成都、曼谷的航班。西双版纳机场在景洪市南 6 千米处。

也可以坐汽车去云南各地及周边省份。

2010 年 10 月，当地宣布，计划建设一条长达 530 千米的铁路，把西双版纳和老挝万象连接起来；西双版纳和泰国之间通车也是很有可能的。

参考答案

Section I：Dialog

导游：凯文，您好。这是您第一次来青岛吗？

游客：Yes, the very first.

导游：那么，欢迎到青岛来。

游客：Thanks. Linda, you know, I won't be here for long. Is there anything worth seeing here?

导游：海边。应该说，那是游客必去之地。

游客：The coast? I know Qingdao is surrounded by water on three sides and backed by the mountains. Is there anything special about the coast?

导游：当然。青岛最美的景区就在沿海一线。

游客：Really? I'd like to hear that.

导游：先说栈桥吧。栈桥始建于 1891 年，是个军用码头。1897 年，德国占领青岛后，把它变成了货运码头。如今，它变成了这个城市的象征。都说，没到过栈桥，不算来过青岛。

游客：Really? German occupation? No wonder Qingdao, when seen from above, looks like a German city.

导游：是的。栈桥也许是青岛游人最多的地方。在那里，如果幸运的话，还可以看到人们喂海鸥的情景。

游客：Seagulls? Oh, the harmony between Man and Nature!

导游：沿着海滨走去，您会发现很多旅游景点，如上面有个灯塔的小青岛、可以饱览市容的小鱼山、海军博物馆、水族馆、青岛六大海水浴场之一也是亚洲最大的海水浴场——青岛第一海水浴场、奥帆基地、万国建筑博览群、极地海洋世界等。

游客：Sounds good. I just can't wait.

导游：值得特别一提的是海滨木栈道。全长 36.9 千米，自西而东，经过 7 大景区。

游客：So you can enjoy what the locals call "red roofs, green trees, blue seas and clear skies".

导游：千真万确。沿途宁静的公园、阳光沙滩与喧嚣的城市形成了鲜明对比。

游客：Yes, I can imagine. What a happy life the locals live!

导游：那还等什么？还不赶快去领略沿途的风景。

游客：OK, let's.

Section Ⅱ：Passage

阿姆斯特丹

阿姆斯特丹是荷兰的首都。其首都地位是由荷兰宪法所规定的，尽管它不是荷兰政府的所在地。荷兰政府的所在地是海牙。

阿姆斯特丹位于荷兰西部的北荷兰省。阿姆斯特尔河在市中心流入很多运河，这些运河最终汇入 IJ 湾。阿姆斯特丹位于海平面以下 2 米。周围的土地是平的，由大片的围垦地构成。西南部是一片人造林。阿姆斯特丹通过长长的北海运河与北海相连。

作为荷兰的商业、文化首都以及欧洲最大的金融中心之一，阿姆斯特丹被"全球化和世界城市研究小组"认为是最重要的国际都市。荷兰很多大型机构的总部设在这里，7 家世界 500 强公司的总部也在这里。

阿姆斯特丹的运河总长 100 多千米。在中世纪时，阿姆斯特丹周边有一条护城河，现在成为该市最内侧的一环，使市中心呈马蹄铁状。该市还有一个海港。阿姆斯特丹由约 90 个岛屿组成，岛与岛之间由 1200 多座桥梁连接，因此，阿姆斯特丹通常又有"北方威尼斯"之称。

阿姆斯特丹的运河系统是城市规划的结果。在 17 世纪早期移民潮达到顶峰的时候，出台了一个全面的计划，即所有运河按照 4 个同心半圆排开，最终流入 IJ 湾。运河的作用有三：国防、水资源管理和运输。

阿姆斯特丹是欧洲最受欢迎的旅游目的地之一，每年接待 463 万以上国际游客，这还不包括每年 1600 万当天往返的游客。游客的数量在过去 10 年里稳步增长，这是因为欧洲游客越来越多。三分之二的酒店位于市中心。四星级或五星级酒店提供了床位总数的 42%，外加只在阿姆斯特丹过夜的床位的 41%。2006 年，房间入住率为 78%，比 2005 年增加了 8 个百分点。大多数游客来自欧洲，占 74%。最大的非欧洲旅游团来自美国，占总数的 14%。阿姆斯特丹在某些年份里会推出某个主题，吸引更多的游人。这个时候，一些酒店会做出特殊安排或推出特殊活动。城市周围有4个营地，每年到这里旅游的人数从12000到65000不等。

Section Ⅲ: Passage

Xishuangbanna

Xishuangbanna, or *Sipsongpanna*, is an autonomous prefecture in the south of Yunnan Province in southern China. The prefectural seat is Jinghong, the largest settlement in the area and one that straddles the Lancang River.

Sipsongpanna is a Tai Lü (or Dai language) compound consisting of *sipsong* meaning "twelve", and *panna* meaning "1000 *mu* or about 67 hectares of rice fields". The name refers to the traditional division of the *mueang*, or semi-independent city—states or principalities, into twelve districts that were called *panna*.

The prefecture has an area of 19,700 km^2. Xishuangbanna is the home of the Dai people. The region sits at a lower altitude than most of Yunnan, and borders closely on tropical climate. It is fast becoming a sought after tourist destination.

Xishuangbanna harbors much of the biodiversity of Yunnan Province, which harbors much of the biodiversity of China. Its tropical climate and its remoteness until recent times accounts for this. In addition to an abundance of plants, Xishuangbanna is home to the last few Asian elephants still in China, the species roaming over a large part of the country even as late as a few hundred years ago. The elephants are protected in a reserve, but the plant diversity is threatened by the proliferation of rubber plantations which completely destroy the rainforest and replace it with a monoculture of trees originally from Brazil.

The six famous tea mountains region, located in the prefecture, produce some of the most highly regarded Pu-erh tea in the 20th century.

Xishuangbanna is rich in natural, historical and cultural resources, noted for its folklore, rain forests, rare plants and wildlife. Its major tourist attractions include Manfeilong Pagodas, Jingzhen Octagonal Pavilion, Wild Elephant Gully, and Dai people's village at Ganlanba. What is worth special mentioning is Xishuangbanna Tropical Botanical Garden. Founded in 1959, the Chinese Academy of Sciences-affiliated research institution engaged in biodiversity conservation and sustainable uses of plant resources, is located in Mengla County, Xishuangbanna, covering an area of 1125 hectares. Over 13,000 species of tropical plants are preserved in its 35 living collections.

The well-known traditional festival is the ethnic Dai's Water-Splashing Festival. It lasts for three days from April 13 to 15. Besides the water festival event it also consists of some other events such as Dragon boat races, firing of indigenous missiles, flying Kongming Lamps.

Since the opening of the Xishuangbanna Gasa Airport (formerly "Jinghong International Airport") in 1990, traveling to Xishuangbanna by air has become more popular and convenient and there are daily flights connecting Xishuangbanna with the city of Kunming. The area also has air connections with Dali, Chengdu and Bangkok. The Xishuangbanna Airport is 6 kilometers south of the city of Jinghong.

There are also bus routes to places all over Yunnan and neighboring provinces.

In October 2010, plans were announced for a 530-kilometer railway linking Xishuangbanna to Vientiane, Laos; connections to Thailand are also possible.

课文 2　Text B

Section Ⅰ: Dialog

Interpret the following dialog alternatively into English and Chinese.

导游: Good morning, Mr. Smith. My name is Wang, Dachuan Wang. My English name is Max. So you can call me Max. I'm your tour guide today. I hope you had a good sleep last night.

游客: 谢谢，麦克斯。我睡得很好。我的气色如何？

导游: You look great. You are in great shape indeed.

游客: 我每天都健身。对了，今天您带我去游览市容，对吧？

导游: Yes, you are right. I was wondering if you already knew anything about Luoyang before you came.

游客: 皮毛而已。我知道，它是一个古老的城市，是九朝古都。这里的牡丹花很有名。

导游: That's not bad. Look, this is the Peony Square, the largest square in the city.

游客: 噢，好大啊。看，草啊、树啊，多绿啊。那边还有个音乐喷泉呢。

导游: Right. The road we are walking on is called Zhongzhou Road. It is 15 kilometers long, and it passes through the city from the west to the east. The plane trees along both sides of the road are about 50 years old. They give us a lot of shade in summer.

游客：那是。噢，我看到很多牡丹花。难道这就是网上说的王城公园吗？

导游：Exactly. The Peony Festival is held here once a year. And the peonies here in Luoyang are said to be the best under the sun.

游客：看出来了，您真为自己的家乡感到自豪啊。

导游：Aren't you? Here we are at Luoyang Museum, which houses one tenths of the unearthed relics in China. And the most well-known ones are the tricolored ceramics of the Tang Dynasty.

游客：这么多啊？ 想都不敢想！

导游：Now we are standing right in the center of the city. Here you can see the Capital Square, Luoyang Department Store, Luoyang Glass Factory, the largest float glass production base in Asia.

游客：从某种意义上来说，洛阳市是个工业城市。

导游：This is absolutely true. Now we have come to Dingding Road. *Dingding* means to establish the capital. It used to be the main road leading to the Imperial Palace of the Tang Dynasty about a thousand years ago. It was as wide as 141 meters, even wider than the Chang'an Boulevard in today's Beijing. It is not far from here that Empress Wu Zetian, the only empress in Chinese history, ascended the throne.

游客：所以，洛阳作为历史名城此言不虚。

导游：Now you can see the Nine-Dragon Quadripod, reminding people that Luoyang used to be the capital city of 9 dynasties.

游客：有意思。

导游：Finally, we'll round off today's tour with a visit to the Former Residence of Laocius, a philosopher in the Spring and Autumn Period and founder of Taoism.

游客：今天真是不虚此行啊。多谢。

Section II: Passage
Interpret the following passage into Chinese.

Shedd Aquarium

Shedd Aquarium is an indoor public aquarium in Chicago, Illinois in the United States that opened on May 30, 1930. The aquarium contains over 25,000 fish, and was for some time the largest indoor aquarium in the world with 5,000,000

US gallons of water. Shedd Aquarium was the first inland aquarium with a permanent saltwater fish collection. It has 2 million annual visitors; it was the most visited aquarium in the U.S. in 2005, and in 2007, it surpassed the Field Museum as the most popular cultural attraction in Chicago. It contains 1500 species including fish, marine mammals, birds, snakes, amphibians, and insects.

The aquarium cost \$3,000,000 to build, and initially included 132 exhibit tanks. Groundbreaking took place on November 2, 1927, and construction was completed on December 19, 1929; the first exhibits were opened on May 30, 1930.

There are several permanent exhibits at the Shedd: Waters of the World, Caribbean Reef, Amazon Rising, Wild Reef, Stingray Touch and the Abbott Oceanarium.

The oldest galleries in the aquarium feature exhibits on Oceans, Rivers, Islands and Lakes, and Chicago's own Local Waters.

The Caribbean Reef exhibit was built in 1971, on the site of the aquarium's very first exhibit, the Tropical Pool. A feature of this exhibit is a diver that interacts with the animals while talking with the people. A part of the exhibit is a 90,000-US-gallon circular tank that allows for maximum walk-around viewing. The tank is near the center of the first floor.

The Amazon Rising exhibit is an 800 m^2 walkthrough flooded forest recreation of the Amazon River and the surrounding jungle. This exhibit contains 250 different species, and its highest water level is 1.8 meters.

In 2003 Shedd opened Wild Reef, a permanent exhibit located two levels below the main building. The 750,000-US-gallon exhibit recreates a Philippine coral. The main draw of this attraction is a 400,000-US-gallon shark exhibit with 3.7-meter high curved windows, allowing visitors a diver's-eye view. The Wild Reef exhibit also features a saltwater tank display area where coral is propagated and grown for conservation purposes.

In 1991, Shedd Aquarium opened the Oceanarium, a large addition to the aquarium that features marine mammals, including sea otters and California sea lions, as well as penguins. It is, in fact, the largest indoor marine mammal facility in the world.

The Daniel P. Haerther Center for Conservation and Research helps to provide on-site research at the aquarium. They study topics such as animal health and behavior, nutrition, animal training, reproduction and genetics. The research done at the Shedd can be used to provide unique insight on conservation efforts around the world.

Section Ⅲ：Passage
Interpret the following passage into English.

洛 杉 矶

洛杉矶是美国加州人口最多的城市，也是美国人口第二大城市，仅次于纽约。据2010年的美国人口普查，洛杉矶的人口总数为3792621人。

洛杉矶位于加州南部，土地面积1215平方千米，也是洛杉矶县的政府所在地。洛杉矶县是美国人口最稠密的地方，也是美国种族最多样化的县之一。当然，整个洛杉矶地区也被认为是美国最多元化的大都市。该市的居民叫作"洛杉矶人"。

洛杉矶地形不规则，地面平坦，亦有丘陵。城市的最高点是路肯斯山，海拔5074英尺（1547米），位于圣费尔南多谷的东北方。洛杉矶河基本上是一条季节性河流，是主要的排水渠道。

洛杉矶属于亚热带地中海气候，全年阳光明媚，可测量的降水平均每年只有35天。市中心的年平均气温是白天19到24摄氏度，晚上14摄氏度。在最冷的1月，白天温度通常为15到23摄氏度，晚上为7到13摄氏度。在最热的8月，白天温度通常为26到32摄氏度，晚上为18摄氏度左右。

洛杉矶地区有着丰富的本地植物，这在一定程度上要归因于栖息地的多样性，包括海滩、湿地和山脉。许多本地物种（如洛杉矶向日葵）已经变得非常罕见，被认为是濒危物种。洛杉矶的市树是珊瑚树，尽管它不是本地物种；洛杉矶的市花是天堂鸟。

洛杉矶的昵称是"天使之城"。这是一个全球化的城市，其优势表现在商业、国际贸易、娱乐、文化、媒体、时尚、科学、体育、科技、教育、医学和研究等领域，在全球城市指数中排名第六，在全球经济力量指数中排名第九。该市是著名机构的所在地，涵盖专业和文化领域的方方面面，是美国最重要的经济引擎之一。

洛杉矶在电视作品、电子游戏、录制音乐、电影制作方面领先于世界。此外，洛杉矶分别于1932年和1984年举办了夏季奥运会。

参考答案

Section Ⅰ：Dialog

导游：史密斯先生，早上好。 我姓王，叫王大川。 我的英语名字叫麦克斯，所以，您可以叫我麦克斯。 我是您今天的导游。 希望您昨晚睡得很好。

游客：Thanks, Max. I did. How do I look?

导游：您气色很好。您身体的确很棒。

游客：I work out every day. By the way, you'll take me out on a tour of the city today, right?

导游：对。我想知道，您来洛阳之前对这个城市有所了解吗？

游客：Not much. I know, it's an ancient city, and it used to be the capital of 9 dynasties. Besides, it's known for its peonies.

导游：不错嘛。瞧，这就是牡丹广场，也是市里最大的广场。

游客：Oh, so huge. Look, the grass, the trees—how green they are. There's even a music fountain over there.

导游：没错。我们走的这条路叫"中州路"，全长15千米，横穿洛阳市的东西。路两旁的梧桐树都有50年左右的树龄，夏天树荫很大。

游客：Naturally. Oh, I see many peonies. Is this the Capital Garden on the internet?

导游：正是。一年一度的牡丹花会就在这里举办。人们都说，"洛阳牡丹甲天下"。

游客：I can see that you are very proud of your city.

导游：谁不是啊？现在，我们到了洛阳博物馆，这里珍藏着中国十分之一的出土文物。其中，最著名的是唐三彩。

游客：So many? Unthinkable, isn't it?

导游：现在，我们来到市中心。您可以看到王城广场、洛阳百货商店以及洛阳玻璃厂。洛阳玻璃厂是亚洲最大的浮法玻璃生产基地。

游客：In a sense, Luoyang is an industrial city.

导游：的确如此。现在，我们来到定鼎路。"定鼎"就是定都的意思。这里曾经是1000多年前唐朝宫城的正街，宽141米，比今天北京的长安街还要宽。不远处，就是中国历史上唯一的女皇帝武则天登基的地方。

游客：So it is rightly said that Luoyang is a famous cultural and historic city.

导游：现在您看到的是九龙鼎，提醒人们洛阳曾是九朝古都。

游客：Interesting.

导游：最后，我们参观一下老子的故居，然后结束今天的游览。老子是春秋时期的哲学家，也是道教学派的创始人。

游客：This is really a rewarding trip. Thanks a million.

Section Ⅱ：Passage

谢德水族馆

谢德水族馆是美国伊利诺斯州芝加哥市的一个室内公共水族馆，于1930年5月30日对外营业。馆内有2.5万多条鱼，一度是世界上最大的室内水族馆，有

500万美制加仑水。谢德水族馆是第一个内陆水族馆,里面永久性地收集了很多咸水鱼。水族馆每年接待200万游客;它是2005年美国参观人数最多的水族馆。2007年,它超越了芝加哥的菲尔德博物馆,成为芝加哥最受欢迎的文化景点。馆内有1500种生物,包括鱼、海洋哺乳动物、鸟、蛇、两栖动物和昆虫等。

水族馆耗资300万美元,起初包括132个展缸。1927年11月2日破土动工,1929年12月19日建成。首批展品于次年5月30日对公众开放。

谢德水族馆有几个永久性的展品:世界的水域、加勒比海珊瑚礁、涨水期的亚马逊河、野生礁、走近黄貂鱼和阿尔伯特海洋水族馆。

馆内最古老的长廊展出的是海洋、河流、岛屿、湖泊以及芝加哥当地的水域。

加勒比海珊瑚礁展于1971年建在水族馆的第一个展品——热带池原址上。该展览的一大特点是,一名潜水员在与人交谈的同时,与动物亲密接触。展览的一部分是一个容积为9万美制加仑的圆缸,游人可以最大限度地在展缸外绕行欣赏。该展缸几乎位于一楼的中央。

涨水期的亚马逊河展占地800平方米,再现了亚马逊河旁淹没了的森林和周边的原始丛林。这个展览包含了250种不同的物种,最高水位为1.8米。

2003年,谢德水族馆对外推出野生礁展,这是一个永久性的展览,位于水族馆的负二层。这个容积为75万美制加仑的展览再现了菲律宾珊瑚的风貌。该展览最吸引人的地方是一个容积为40万美制加仑的鲨鱼展览,有一个3.7米高的拱窗,让游客像潜水员一样去欣赏。野生礁展还有一个盐水缸展区,供珊瑚繁殖成长,以便观察研究。

1991年,谢德水族馆推出了海洋水族馆,这是对水族馆展品的极大补充,主要有海洋哺乳动物(包括海獭和加州海狮)和企鹅。事实上,它是世界上最大的室内海洋哺乳动物水族馆。

丹尼尔·P·希瑟尔保护研究中心协助水族馆进行现场研究。他们研究的主题包括动物健康和行为、营养、动物训练、繁殖和遗传等。谢德水族馆的研究可以为世界各地的保护工作提供独到的视角。

Section Ⅲ: Passage

Los Angeles

Los Angeles is the most populous city in the U. S. State of California and the second most populous city in the United States, after New York City, with a population of 3,792,621 at the 2010 United States Census.

Located in Southern California, Los Angeles, with a land area of 1,215 km^2, is also the seat of Los Angeles County, the most populated and one of the most ethnically diverse counties in the United States, while the entire Los Angeles area itself has been recognized as the most diverse of the nation's largest cities. The city's inhabitants are referred to as Angelenos.

Los Angeles, irregularly shaped, is both flat and hilly. The highest point in the city is 5,074 ft (1,547 m) Mount Lukens, located at the northeastern end of the San Fernando Valley. The Los Angeles River, which is largely seasonal, is the primary drainage channel.

Los Angeles has a Subtropical-Mediterranean climate. It has plenty of sunshine throughout the year, with an average of only 35 days with measurable precipitation annually. The average annual temperature in downtown is 19℃ to 24℃ during the day and 14℃ at night. In the coldest month January, the temperature typically ranges from 15℃ to 23℃ during the day and 7℃ to 13℃ at night. In the warmest month, August, the temperature typically ranges from 26℃ to 32℃ during the day and around 18℃ at night.

The Los Angeles area is rich in native plant species due in part to a diversity in habitats, including beaches, wetlands, and mountains. Many of these native species, such as the Los Angeles sunflower, have become so rare as to be considered endangered. Though it is not native to the area, the official tree of Los Angeles is the Coral Tree and the official flower of Los Angeles is the Bird of Paradise.

Nicknamed the City of Angels, Los Angeles is a global city, with strengths in business, international trade, entertainment, culture, media, fashion, science, sports, technology, education, medicine and research and has been ranked sixth in the Global Cities Index and 9th Global Economic Power Index. The city is home to renowned institutions covering a broad range of professional and cultural fields and is one of the most substantial economic engines within the United States.

Los Angeles leads the world in the creation of television productions, video games, recorded music and motion picture production. Additionally, Los Angeles hosted the Summer Olympic Games in 1932 and 1984.

第5单元
饭店就餐

Eating Out

课文 1　Text A

Section Ⅰ: Dialog
Interpret the following dialog alternatively into English and Chinese.

服务员：Good evening, sir? How many are there in your party, please?

客人：晚上好。4位。

服务员：Do you prefer to sit by the window or by the aisle?

客人：有单间吗?

服务员：Sorry, sir. We are all booked up for tonight.

客人：那就找个安静的角落吧。

服务员：OK, sir. This way, please.

客人：谢谢。嗯，有菜单吗？ 嗯，不，请问，你们这儿有什么特色菜吗?

服务员：I recommend steaks. It is no exaggeration to say that they are a must for foodies.

客人：那好，就来四份牛排吧。

服务员：How would you like them to be cooked, sir?

客人：一份全熟，一份七分熟，一份四分熟，一份一分熟。

服务员：One for well done, one for medium well, one for medium rare and one for blue rare. OK, anything else, sir?

客人：要4个煎蛋。

服务员：How would you like them to be served, sir?

客人：一个煎得老一点，其余的煎得嫩一点。

服务员：One for sunny side down, and the rest for sunny side up. Good. Would you like anything to drink, sir?

客人：一杯啤酒，一大杯可乐，两杯水。

服务员：Is that all, sir?

客人：是的。能快点吗？ 我们赶时间。

服务员：Don't worry, sir. I'll rush them for you.

客人：多谢。

服务员：My pleasure. We'll bring them to you right away.

Section II: Passage
Interpret the following passage into Chinese.

Table Manners (Part One)

Table manners are the rules of etiquette used while eating, which may also include the appropriate use of utensils. Different cultures observe different rules for table manners. Each family or social group sets its own standards for how strictly these rules are to be enforced.

Now let's look at the table manners in the United Kingdom.

In the UK, it is standrad practice for the host or hostess to take the first bite. The host begins after all food is served and everyone is seated. Food should always be tasted before salt and pepper are added. Applying condiments or seasoning before the food is tasted is viewed as an insult to the cook, as it shows a lack of faith in his/her ability to prepare a meal. In religious households, a family meal may commence with saying Grace, or at dinner parties the guests might begin the meal by offering some favorable comments on the food and thanks to the host. In a group dining situation it is considered impolite to begin eating before all the group have been served their food and are ready to start.

The fork is held with the left hand and the knife held with the right. The fork is held generally with the tines down, using the knife to cut food or help guide food on to the fork. When no knife is being used, the fork can be held with the tines up. Under no circumstances should the fork be held like a shovel, with all fingers wrapped around the base. With the tines up, the fork balances on the side of the index finger, held in place with the thumb and index finger. When eating soup, the spoon is held in the right han, scooping the soup in outward movements. The soup spoon should never be put into your mouth, and soup should be sipped from the side of the spoon, not the end. Your knife must never enter your mouth or be licked. Food should always be chewed with the mouth closed. Talking with food in your mouth is seen as very rude. Licking one's fingers and eating slowly can also be considered not polite.

On formal dining occasions, it is OK to take some butter from the butter dish with your bread knife and put it on your side plate (for the roll). Then butter pieces of the roll using this butter. This prevents the butter in the dish getting full of bread crumbs as it is passed around. Knives should be used to butter bread rolls but not to cut them—tear off a mouthful at a time with your hands.

All wine, red, white and sparkling, is held by the stem of the glass. Wines should be served in the sequence "white before red, light before heavy, young before old". Pouring your own drink when eating with other people is acceptable, but it is more polite to offer pouring drinks to the people sitting on either side of you.

It is impolite to reach over someone to pick up food or other items. Diners should always ask for items to be passed along the table to them. In the same vein, diners should pass those items directly to the person who asked. It is also rude to slurp food, eat noisily or make noise with cutlery.

When you've finished eating, and to let others know that you have, place your knife and fork together (fork on the left), with the prongs (tines) on the fork facing upwards, on your plate. Napkins should be placed unfolded on the table when the meal is finished.

At family meals, children are often expected to ask permission to leave the table at the end of the meal.

Section Ⅲ: Passage
Interpret the following passage into English.

慕尼黑啤酒节

慕尼黑啤酒节,也叫十月节,是世界上最大的公共节日,于 2013 年举办了第 180 届。每年,约有 600 万游客参加啤酒节,喝掉约 500 万升啤酒,吃掉无数猪肉香肠。这些美酒佳肴主要是在慕尼黑传统啤酒厂搭建的"啤酒大篷"里消费的。

在啤酒节巨大的场地上,还有旋转木马、过山车以及各种各样令人亢奋的娱乐活动,让所有年龄的人们去享受,去狂欢。

啤酒节的历史可以追溯到 19 世纪。路德维希王储,即后来的国王路德维希一世,于 1810 年 10 月 12 日娶了泰瑞莎公主。慕尼黑的市民应邀参加在城门前空地上举办的庆典,庆祝皇家的大喜之事。

当着皇室的面举办赛马活动,标志着整个巴伐利亚庆典活动的闭幕。有关次年再次举办赛马活动的决定催生了慕尼黑啤酒节的传统。

1811 年,除了赛马以外,又新添了一大特色——农业展,旨在促进巴伐利亚农业发展。赛马曾是啤酒节上最古老、最受欢迎的活动,于今已不再举行。但是,农业展仍然是每 3 年在啤酒节场地的南部举行 1 次。

在最初的几十年里,娱乐项目并不多见。1818 年,第 1 次出现了一个旋转木马和两个秋千。游客可以在小啤酒摊上喝酒止渴,后来小啤酒摊的数量迅速增加。

1896年，啤酒摊被首批啤酒大篷和啤酒大厅所取代。这些帐篷和大厅都是由啤酒厂搭建的。

啤酒节场地的其他部分成了游乐场。旋转木马的数量种类在19世纪70年代迅速增加，这是德国广场贸易不断增长的结果。

如今，慕尼黑啤酒节已经发展成为蔚为壮观的盛事。2013年，142个饮食摊位和173家串演单位在大约85英亩的场地上提供食品、饮料和娱乐活动。如今，东道主巴伐利亚人正期待700万人从世界各地来这里饮酒作乐。

2010年，出现了一个具有历史意义的展览会，其目的是为让游客重温传统啤酒节的味道。它为附近庞大喧闹的啤酒节提供了另一种选择，尤其是针对那些有孩子、有老人的家庭。它聚焦于巴伐利亚的风土人情、慕尼黑人的热情好客和传统的民间音乐。传统的节日大篷就是一个很好的例子，通过美味佳肴和传统服装展示给人以实实在在的感觉。2013年，又增加了有机食品，如烤鸡、荤菜等。此外，还首次出现了素食菜肴。

总之，慕尼黑啤酒节是在德国巴伐利亚省慕尼黑市举办的一年一度的嘉年华，也是世界上最大的。这是一个为期16天的节日，从9月下旬持续到10月份的第1个周末。每年，有600多万人从世界各地赶来参加庆典。这是巴伐利亚文化的一个重要组成部分。

参考答案

Section I：Dialog

服务员：先生，晚上好。请问，一共几位？

客人：Good evening. We are a party of four.

服务员：您是坐靠窗户的位子，还是靠过道的位子？

客人：Is there a private room for us?

服务员：对不起，先生。今晚的单间都订出去了。

客人：Get us a quiet corner then.

服务员：好的，先生。这边请。

客人：Thank you. Well, do you have a menu？Oh no. What do you recommend?

服务员：牛排。毫不夸张地说，牛排是美食家必选的。

客人：In that case, four steaks, please.

服务员：都要几分熟的，先生？

客人：One for well done, one for medium well, one for medium rare and one for blue rare.

服务员：一份全熟，一份七分熟，一份四分熟，一份一分熟。好的，还要别的吗，先生？

客人：Four fried eggs, please.

服务员：要老一点的，还是嫩一点的，先生？

客人：One for sunny side down, and the rest for sunny side up.

服务员：一个煎得老一点，其余的煎得嫩一点。好的。要喝点什么吗，先生？

客人：A glass of beer, a large coke, and two glasses of water.

服务员：就这么多吗，先生？

客人：Yes. Could you rush them for us? We are in a big hurry.

服务员：放心吧，先生。我会催的。

客人：Thanks a lot.

服务员：不客气。马上就好。

Section Ⅱ：Passage

餐桌礼仪（第一部分）

餐桌礼仪是就餐时需要遵守的礼仪规则，其中也包括正确使用餐具。不同文化有不同的餐桌礼仪。每一个家庭、每一个社团对如何严格遵守这些礼仪都有自己的标准。

现在让我们来看看英国的餐桌礼仪。

在英国，通常是男主人或女主人先吃第一口。待上菜完毕、所有人都落座后，主人就开始了。在加盐和胡椒面之前，一定要先品尝一下食物。在没有品尝食物之前竟自添加调料被视为是对厨师的侮辱，因为那意味着对主人的烹饪技术抱怀疑态度。在宗教家庭里，一家人吃饭前要做谢饭祷告；在宴会上，客人在吃饭前会称赞一下食物，感谢一下主人。在很多人一起聚会时，在所有人面前都摆好了食物、都准备开始之前贸然进食，被认为是有失体统的。

左手叉，右手刀。叉子一般是尖头朝下。用刀切割食物，或把食物弄到叉子上。不用刀时，叉尖可以朝上。在任何情况下，都不能像拿铁锹一样拿叉子，不能用所有指头握住叉子把儿。叉尖朝上时，叉子靠食指内侧平衡，即拇指和食指一起用力。喝汤时，右手拿汤匙，由内往外舀。汤匙永远不要放进嘴里，从汤匙边上小口喝汤，而不是对着勺子尖喝。刀也永远不能放进嘴里，也不能用舌头舔。咀嚼食物时，要闭着嘴。嘴里含着食物说话被看成是非常粗鲁的。舔手指、慢吞吞地进食都被认为是不礼貌的。

在正式用餐场合，可以用面包刀从黄油盘里取一些黄油，放在旁边的小盘子里，以便吃餐包时用。接着，把黄油涂抹到餐包上，这样，可以防止在传递面包的过程中把面包屑撒在黄油上。刀子是用来涂抹餐包的，而不是来切餐包的。餐包要用手撕，一次一小口。

所有的葡萄酒，无论是红葡萄酒、白葡萄酒，还是起泡葡萄酒，喝的时候都要握住杯柄。喝葡萄酒的顺序应该是"先白，后红，先度数低的，后度数高的，先年头短的，后年头长的"。与他人一起进餐时，可以给自己倒酒。不过，主动给身边的人倒酒则显得更有礼貌。

越过别人的身体去夹取食物或其他东西是不礼貌的。永远都要让别人递给你。同样，必要时，你也要把食物等递给别人。吃东西时吧嗒吧嗒、咕噜咕噜，或者把餐具弄得叮当作响，也都是极不礼貌的。

用餐完毕，或者想让别人知道你吃完了，把刀叉一起放在盘子里，叉子放在左边，叉子尖朝上。吃完后，餐巾应该展开放在桌子上。

家庭聚餐时，孩子们要想离开餐桌，需要征得大人的许可。

Section Ⅲ: Passage

The Munich Oktoberfest

The Munich Oktoberfest, also known as the Oktoberfest, is the biggest public festival in the world and was held in 2013 for the 180th time. Each year, the Oktoberfest is attended by around 6 million visitors, who drink around 5 million liters of beer and consume countless pork sausages—mostly in the "beer tents" put up by the traditional Munich breweries.

The huge Oktoberfest grounds also provide carousels, roller coasters and all the spectacular fun of the fair for the enjoyment and excitement of visitors of all ages.

The history of the Oktoberfest dates back to the 19th century. Crown Prince Ludwig, later to become King Ludwig I, was married to Princess Therese on October 12, 1810. The citizens of Munich were invited to attend the festivities held on the fields in front of the city gates to celebrate the happy royal event.

Horse races in the presence of the Royal Family marked the close of the event that was celebrated as a festival for the whole of Bavaria. The decision to repeat the horse races in the subsequent year gave rise to the tradition of the Oktoberfest.

In 1811, an added feature to the horse races was the first Agricultural Show, designed to boost Bavarian agriculture. The horse races, which were the oldest and the most popular event of the festival are no longer held today. But the Agricultural Show is still held every three years during the Oktoberfest on the southern part of the festival grounds.

In the first few decades the choice of amusements was sparse. The first carousel and two swings were set up in 1818. Visitors were able to quench their thirst at small beer stands which grew rapidly in number later. In 1896 the beer stands were replaced by the first beer tents and halls set up by the breweries.

The remainder of the festival site was taken up by a fun-fair. The range of carousels on offer was already increasing rapidly in the 1870s as the fairground trade continued to grow and develop in Germany.

Today, the Munich Oktoberfest has developed into a spectacular event of superlatives: in 2013, 142 caterers and 173 sideshow operators offer food, drinks and entertainment in an area of around 85 acres. The Bavarian hosts are expecting seven million fun-loving guests from around the globe.

In 2010, a historical fair was founded to provide visitors with nostalgic impressions of the traditional Oktoberfest. It offers an alternative to the huge razzmatazz of the neighboring Oktoberfest, especially for families with children and older people. It focuses on Bavarian customs, Munich's hospitality and traditional folk music. The traditional festival tent is a good illustration: it adds an air of authenticity with tasty delicacies and traditional costume displays. In 2013, the choice includes organically produced food, such as grilled chicken and meat dishes, plus vegan dishes for the first time.

In short, Oktoberfest is the world's largest fun fair held annually in Munich, Bavaria, Germany. It is a 16-day festival running from late September to the first weekend in October with more than 6 million people from around the world attending the event every year. It is an important part of Bavarian culture.

课文 2　Text B

Section Ⅰ: Dialog
Interpret the following dialog alternatively into English and Chinese.

店员: Afternoon, Miss. Are you ready to order now?
客人: 能再给我几分钟吗?
店员: No problem. Take your time.
客人: 好了，我要一个汉堡。

店员：Anything else?

客人：一个小薯条，一个大可乐。嗯，再要一个奶昔吧。

店员：What flavor would you like, Miss?

客人：香草味的。

店员：Is that for here or to go?

客人：在这儿吃。

店员：Is that all?

客人：是的。

店员：OK. That will be 40 yuan 50.

客人：糟了，现金不够了。请问，这里可以刷卡吗？

店员：Yes, we do. ...OK. Here's your card, Miss.

客人：谢谢。对了，能多给些番茄酱吗？

店员：Sure. Here you are.

客人：能多给点餐巾纸吗？

店员：Sure.

客人：谢谢。

店员：You are welcome. There you go. Next. Who's next?

客人：噢，来了。

Section Ⅱ：Passage
Interpret the following passage into Chinese.

Table Manners (Part Two)

Having talked about table manners in the UK, now let's move on to those in North America.

Modern etiquette provides the smallest numbers and types of utensils necessary for dining. Only utensils which are to be used for the planned meal should be set. Even if needed, hosts should not have more than three utensils on either side of the plate before a meal. If extra utensils are needed, they may be brought to the table along with later courses.

A table cloth extending 10-15 inches past the edge of the table should be used for formal dinners, while placemats may be used for breakfast, lunch, and informal suppers. Candlesticks, even if not lit, should not be on the table while dining during daylight hours.

Men's and unisex hats should never be worn at the table. Ladies' hats may be worn during the day if visiting others.

Phones and other distracting items should not be used at the dining table. Reading at a table is permitted only at breakfast, unless the diner is alone. Urgent matters should be handled, after an apology, by stepping away from the table.

If food must be removed from the mouth for some reason—a pit, bone, or gristle—the rule of thumb according to Emily Post, is that it comes out the same way it went in. For example, if olives are eaten by hand, the pit may be removed by hand. If an olive in a salad is eaten with a fork, deposit the pit back onto the fork inside your mouth and deposit it on your plate. This is the same with a small bone or piece of gristle—to the fork, to the plate. A diner should never spit things into a napkin, certainly not a cloth napkin. Since the napkin is always laid in the lap and brought up only to wipe one's mouth, hidden food may be dumped into your lap or onto the host's floor. It is further insulting to the server or host to find it there. Food that is simply disliked should be swallowed.

The fork may be used in the American style (in the left hand while cutting and in the right hand to pick up food) or the European Continental style (fork always in the left hand). The napkin should be left on the seat of a chair only when leaving temporarily. Upon leaving the table at the end of a meal, the napkin is placed loosely on the table to the left of the plate.

Section Ⅲ: Passage
Interpret the following passage into English.

美 食 节

美食节是这样一个节日，通常1年举办1次，主题是食物，还常常是农产品。美食节，作为庆祝丰收、感恩生长季节的节日，一直都是睦邻友好的一种手段。美食节可以追溯到数千年以前。那时，是为了庆祝收获季节和秋分的到来，同时，也是为了祭拜大地之神。

世界上最大的美食节是在伊利诺斯州芝加哥市举办的"舌尖上的芝加哥"。

"舌尖上的芝加哥"，常被称为"舌尖"，是世界上最大的美食节，每年7月中旬在芝加哥格兰特公园举行。这是芝加哥最大的节日。与美食无关的活动包括现场音乐演出。音乐人有当地的艺术家，也有全国知名的艺术家。自2008年以来，芝加哥乡村音乐节不再与"舌尖上的芝加哥"同时举行，目的是为了在秋天举办自己为期2天的活动。

2005年,"舌尖上的芝加哥"吸引了390万游客和70多个食品摊贩。美食节上的食品包括芝加哥比萨、芝加哥热狗、烤肋排、意大利牛肉、麦克斯韦街波兰香肠、伊莱芝士蛋糕以及各种民族美食和地区美食。在2004年为期10天的美食节上,共有359万人前来光顾,收入1233万美元。

2007年,"舌尖上的芝加哥"在历史上第1次受到沙门氏菌疫情的影响,700多人受到感染,12人住院。据报道,此次事件是帕尔斯湾摊位出售的鹰嘴豆泥所致。

2011年,"舌尖上的芝加哥"吸引了235万名游人,比2010年下降了11%。参节的餐馆少挣了不少钱。所有收入共计490万美元,较2010年下降了20%。

这些乏善可陈的统计数据带来了几个变化。该市市长把美食节的举办权从芝加哥公园区移交到了文化事务及特殊事务部,美食节也缩短为5天,举办日期也发生了变化。因此,2012年,"舌尖上的芝加哥"的举办时间为7月11日到7月15日。

2012年,"舌尖上的芝加哥"举办了5天,有36个餐馆参节。同时,新增了15家"弹出式"餐馆,每家餐馆只参节1天。

2013年,"舌尖上的芝加哥"6年来首次盈利。

Section I: Dialog

店员:小姐,下午好。可以点餐了吗?

客人:Can you give me a couple more minutes?

店员:没问题。不着急。

客人:Well, I want a hamburger.

店员:还要别的吗?

客人:A small fries, a large coke, and...a milkshake.

店员:要什么口味的,小姐?

客人:Make it vanilla.

店员:是在这儿吃,还是带走?

客人:That'll be for here.

店员:就这么多吗?

客人:Yes.

店员:好的。一共是40元5角。

客人:Too bad that I'm short of cash. Do you take credit cards?

店员：可以。……好了，小姐，这是您的卡。
客人：Thanks. By the way, can I have extra ketchup?
店员：当然，给。
客人：And more napkins?
店员：可以。
客人：Thanks.
店员：不谢。拿好了。下一位。谁是下一位？
客人：Oh, here I am.

Section Ⅱ：Passage

餐桌礼仪（第二部分）

前面谈到了英国的餐桌礼仪，现在让我们谈谈北美的餐桌礼仪。

现代礼仪为用餐者提供的餐具数量最小，种类最少。只有某一顿饭非用不可的餐具才会摆在桌子上。即便需要，主人也不应该于餐前在盘子两边各摆3件以上的餐具。如果需要额外的餐具，会在后面上菜时一起拿上来。

正式晚宴需要使用台布，长度要在桌子边缘以下10至15英寸，而对于早餐、午餐和非正式晚餐，使用餐盘垫布就可以了。烛台，即使没有点燃，白天用餐时，也不应该放在桌子上。

用餐时，不能戴男士帽子和男女皆宜的帽子。女士白天走亲访友时，可以戴帽子。

电话和其他分散注意力的东西在餐桌上不应使用。只有早餐时，可以在餐桌旁看书。其他场合要看书，必须是一个人用餐。需要处理紧急事务时，要先道歉，然后才能离开桌子。

如果因为某种原因需要把食物从嘴里拿出来，如果核、硬骨或软骨等，按照艾米丽·珀斯特的经验法则，应该是怎么吃进去的，怎么拿出来。例如，如果用手吃橄榄，可以用手把核去掉。如果是用叉子吃沙拉中的一个橄榄，那么，就应该在嘴里用叉子叉住，然后，把它放在盘子里。这对于处理一块小骨头或一块软骨来说，也是一样的。先在嘴里叉住，然后，放在盘子里。就餐者永远都不能把东西吐在餐巾纸上，当然，更不能吐在布餐巾上。由于餐巾总是放在腿上，只可以用来擦嘴巴，掉上去的食物可能会掉到你的膝盖上或主人的地板上。如果这样，这对于上菜的人或主人来说，是更大的侮辱。不喜欢的食物也要咽下去。

叉子可以按美国的风俗使用，即切割食物时用左手拿着，夹取食物时，用右手拿着；也可以按欧陆风俗，即叉子总是拿在左手里。暂时离开时，餐巾应该留在椅子上。吃完饭离开桌子时，餐巾应该松散地放在桌子上，放在盘子的左边。

Section Ⅲ: Passage

Food Festivals

A food festival is a festival, usually held annually, that uses food, often produce, as its central theme. These festivals have always been a means of uniting communities through celebrations of harvests and giving thanks for a plentiful growing season. They can be traced back thousands of years to celebrating the arrival of harvest time, the autumnal equinox, and the honoring of earth gods.

The largest festival in the world is the Taste of Chicago held in Chicago, Illinois.

The Taste of Chicago, mostly known as The Taste, is the world's largest food festival, held annually in mid-July in Chicago in Grant Park. The event is the largest festival in Chicago. Non-food-related events include live music. Musical acts vary from local artists to nationally known artists. Since 2008, The Chicago Country Music Festival no longer occurs simultaneously with Taste of Chicago as it departed the Taste of Chicago for its own two-day festival typically held in the fall.

In 2005, the Taste attracted about 3.9 million people with over 70 food vendors. Foods at the event include Chicago-style pizza, Chicago hot dogs, barbecued ribs, Italian Beef, Maxwell Street Polish Sausage, Eli's Cheesecake, and a variety of ethnic and regional foods. Attendance for the previous record 10-day event, in 2004, was 3.59 million, with \$12.33 million in revenue.

In 2007, for the first time in its history, the Taste of Chicago was affected by a salmonella outbreak that affected over 700 people and led to the hospitalization of 12. The outbreak was reportedly traced to hummus served at the Pars Cove booth.

In 2011, the Taste of Chicago drew 2.35 million visitors, down 11 percent from 2010. Participating restaurants also made less money, \$4.9 million, down 20 percent from 2010.

These lackluster statistics prompted several changes. The mayor transferred power over the event from the Chicago Park District to the Department of Cultural Affairs and Special Events, the event was shortened to 5 days, and the dates were changed so that in 2012, the Taste of Chicago will run from July 11 to July 15.

In 2012, the Taste of Chicago ran for five days and had 36 participating restaurants. It added 15 Pop-Up Restaurants that each served food for one of the five days.

In 2013, the Taste of Chicago turned a profit for the first time in six years.

第6单元
休闲购物

Shopping

课文 1　Text A

Section Ⅰ: Dialog
Interpret the following dialog alternatively into English and Chinese.

售货员：Hello, sir. Are you being served?

顾客：没有。不过，我只是随便看看。

售货员：Go ahead, please.

顾客：谢谢。

售货员：If I can be of any help, please let me know.

顾客：好的。

售货员：If you don't mind, I'd like to tell you that these T-shirts are new arrivals. They are very popular this summer.

顾客：我已经注意到了。

售货员：You can try it on if you happen to like one of them. And the fitting room is over there.

顾客：好，我喜欢这个颜色，但不是我的尺寸。我穿5号的。

售货员：How about the green one? Mmm, it looks great on you and has your name on it.

顾客：很好。我试试去。

售货员：What do you think of it?

顾客：很合适。多少钱一件？

售货员：58 dollars. Please pay at the cashier's desk over there.

顾客：我知道。这件蓝色的我也要了。再次感谢。

售货员：You are lucky. There's a special on these T-shirts, as we are celebrating the 5th anniversary of our shop.

顾客：真的吗？怪不得店里这么多人呢。

售货员：Yes. A penny saved is a penny earned, right?

顾客：没错。这样的话，我多买几件。

售货员：Why not buy some for your family? There are new arrivals for ladies and kids, too.

顾客：这个主意不错。非常感谢。

售货员：I'm at your service at any time.

Section Ⅱ: Passage
Interpret the following passage into Chinese.

The World's Biggest Spenders

As BBC's chief business correspondent Linda Yueh reports, the number of Chinese tourists has grown massively in the last two decades.

Impressively, China accounts for nearly 1 in 10 tourists globally.

This number is set to rise and it shouldn't be surprising since China accounts for one-fifth of the world's population.

Projections are that the 100 million trips taken each year now will double by 2020.

This is with only an estimated 5% of the population holding passports, though that's already more than the population of Britain.

Still, with 1.3 billion people, there's a lot more potential tourists.

Chinese tourists are already the biggest spenders globally. They outspend the Americans and Germans, and even the Russians on a per trip basis.

In 2013, Chinese tourists spent over $100 billion (£59.5bn) and they travel to shop.

Some 80% of Chinese tourists view holidays as shopping trips, as compared with about half for those from the Middle East. And they are keen to leave China to do so in order to find lower prices for luxury goods.

"Stubborn" stomachs

Mr. Zhuang, the chief executive of Qunar, China's largest travel website, says Chinese tourists also leave the country to seek better services in holiday spots.

He says that the Chinese stomach is "stubborn", so travellers will prefer places with good Chinese food as well as local food.

None of this should be surprising given the size and rapid growth of China. What is somewhat astounding is how quickly it's changed.

During the 1990s, my Chinese friends found it difficult to travel abroad. They paid large deposits to designated travel agents who were authorised to take them on group tours, to ensure their return on time.

Simply booking a ticket and hotel online yourself weren't really options for the average Chinese.

How different it is now!

The growth of Chinese tourism offers an opportunity for other countries seeking to attract big spending visitors.

But, for under-developed Chinese tourist sites that are affected by pollution and lagging services, surely there's a missed opportunity for the Chinese themselves.

Section Ⅲ: Passage
Interpret the following passage into English.

奢侈品之恋（第一部分）

就在发达国家的人们削减奢侈品支出维持生计时，大奢侈品品牌正把目光投向了中国新贵鼓鼓的钱包，以促进其珠宝、服装、手包和其他时尚饰品的销售。

2009年发布的"中国奢侈品报告"显示，尽管金融危机使欧美、日本对奢侈品的需求总体呈下降水平，但是，中国的奢侈品市场仍在蓬勃发展。这表明，金融危机对中国经济的影响相对有限。

该报告指出，从2008年初到2009年1月，中国超越美国成为仅次于日本的世界第二大奢侈品消费国，占全球销量的25%。商务部去年9月预测，到2014年，我国将成为世界最大的奢侈品市场，占全球业务的23%。

根据该项报告，尽管中国国内消费者由于全球经济衰退对奢侈品的价格变得更加敏感，但他们对未来仍然充满信心。

报告说，约1000名受访者中，一半以上认为，价格不会影响他们的消费行为；约90%的人认为，他们不会仅仅因为经济疲软而改变自己对奢侈品的偏爱。

中国不断扩大的中产阶级构成了一个重要的消费群体，他们渴望购买奢侈品，也买得起奢侈品。中国小康家庭的数量，即年收入超过36500美元的家庭，在2008年达到160万户，而且，将以每年16%的速度增加。到2015年，将达到440万户，仅次于美国、日本和英国。

该报告引用事实说，"在这样一个经济增长速度极快的市场，人们的消费习惯也会变得很快。"事实是，如今，中国消费者60%的奢侈品是在本土购买的，而几年前，大部分奢侈品都是在海外购买的。

你买什么，你就是什么

中国新兴的中产阶级渴望拥有更多、更好的名牌产品作为社会地位、财富、个性和品味的象征。但是，他们的消费行为不成熟，需要教育和引导。

成熟的奢侈品买家只选择与自己个性和品味相匹配的品牌。与此相反的是，越来越多的中国奢侈品买家只是刚刚步入奢侈品世界，对奢侈品品牌了解甚少。

他们通常重视的是奢侈品的实用价值，如质量、材料、设计或工艺等，而忽略其情感价值。

目前,中国的年轻奢侈品消费者只是兴奋于拥有一定数量的奢侈品。不是每个人都了解奢侈品品牌的不同内涵、历史及其代表的不同生活方式。

此外,对中国的新贵来说,炫耀性消费或多或少是进入一个或多个以财富为唯一衡量标准的俱乐部的敲门砖。

对大多中国人来说,奢侈品代表社会地位和物质财富。也就是说,如果和你收入相当的朋友买了路易威登包,你往往会认为,你也买得起,也应该买一个。

Section Ⅰ: Dialog

售货员:先生,您好。有人招呼您吗?

顾客: Oh no. But I'm just looking around.

售货员:请便。

顾客: Thanks.

售货员:有事您说话。

顾客: OK.

售货员:如果您不介意的话,我倒是想告诉您,这些 T 恤衫全是新款,今年夏天很流行。

顾客: I have noticed that.

售货员:您要是相中了哪一件,不妨试试。试衣间在那边。

顾客: OK. I like the color, but it's not my size. I wear size 5.

售货员:这件绿色的怎么样? 嗯,您穿很好看,就是为您量身定做的。

顾客: Very good. I'll go try it on.

售货员:怎么样?

顾客: It fits me well. How much is it?

售货员:58 美元。请到那边收银台付钱。

顾客: I know. I'll take this blue one, too. Thanks again.

售货员:您很幸运。这些 T 恤衫搞特价,因为今年是我们 5 周年店庆。

顾客: Really? No wonder there are so many people here.

售货员:对呀。省钱就是挣钱嘛。

顾客: Exactly. In that case, I'll buy some more.

售货员:为什么不给家人也买几件呢? 女装、童装也都有新款。

顾客: Capital idea. Thank you very much.

售货员:随时为您效劳。

Section Ⅱ：Passage

全球最大的消费群体

根据英国广播公司（BBC）首席商业记者岳琳达（音译）的报道，中国游客的数量在过去20年里大幅增长。

令人惊叹的是，中国游客占全球总数的10%。

这个数字将会继续增加。这也没有什么可大惊小怪的，因为中国人口占世界总数的五分之一。

现在中国每年有1亿人次出行，到2020年，这个数字预计将翻1倍。

这仅仅是针对5%左右持有护照的人而言的，尽管这个数字已经超过了英国的人口总数。

不过，13亿人口，还有很多潜在的游客。

中国游客已经是全球最大的消费群体。就每一次出行的购物情况来看，他们已经超过了美国人、德国人，甚至还有俄罗斯人。

2013年，中国游客支出了1000多亿美元（595亿英镑）。他们旅行的目的就是购物。

约有80%的中国游客认为，假日就是出去购物，而这一数字在中东也仅有40%。他们之所以喜欢到国外购物，是因为在国外购买奢侈品会便宜很多。

"固执的"胃

中国最大的旅游网站"去哪儿"的首席执行官庄先生说，中国游客之所以到国外，还为了在度假胜地得到更好的服务。

他还说，中国人的胃很"固执"，所以，游客会喜欢提供当地美食和可口中餐的地方。

鉴于中国巨大的面积及经济的快速增长，这一切都没有什么可以感到惊讶的。真正令人惊讶的是，这一变化都来得太快。

20世纪90年代，我的中国朋友发现出国旅行十分困难。为了参加指定旅行社组织的团体旅游，必须交巨额押金以确保他们能按时返回。

那时，自己在网上买票、预订酒店，对普通中国人来说，简直不可想象。

如今，一切都彻底变了。

中国旅游业的发展为其他国家寻求吸引喜欢巨额消费的游客提供了一个机会。

但是，对于污染严重、服务滞后的中国欠发达旅游景点来说，肯定错失了吸引国人的机会。

Section Ⅲ: Passage

A Love Affair with Luxury (Part One)

While people in the developed world are cutting back on luxury items to make ends meet, the big luxury brands are targeting the swelling wallets of China's new money to boost sales of their jewelry, clothing, purses and other lifestyle accessories.

A report on China's luxury goods, released in 2009, showed that while the financial crisis caused general decline in demand for luxury brands in Europe, America and Japan, the Chinese luxury goods market is still thriving, indicating the economic impact of the financial crisis on China is relatively limited.

The report said China surpassed the United States to be the world's second largest luxury goods consumer after Japan, from the beginning of 2008 to January 2009, accounting for 25 percent of global sales. The Ministry of Commerce last September predicted China would become the world's largest luxury market by 2014, accounting for 23 percent of global business.

According to the report, although Chinese domestic consumers became more sensitive to the prices of luxury goods due to the global economic downturn, they're still confident of the future.

The report said more than half of the about 1,000 respondents didn't think the prices will affect their consumption behavior, and nearly 90 percent said that they would not change their preferences for luxury goods just because of the economic weakness.

China's expanding middle class constitutes an important group of consumers who desire and can afford luxury goods. The number of well-off Chinese households, which have more than \$36,500 in annual family income, stood at 1.6 million in 2008 and will grow by 16 percent every year to reach 4.4 million by 2015, next to the United States, Japan and Britain.

"Consumer habits will change fast in a market with such explosive growth," said the report, citing the fact that Chinese customers now buy 60 percent of luxury goods on the mainland, though several years ago they just bought most of their luxury items overseas.

You are what you buy

China's emerging middle class aspires to have more and better designer items as a symbol of social status, wealth, personality and taste, but their consumer behavior is not mature and needs education and guidance.

In contrast to mature luxury buyers who choose only brands matching their personality and taste, a growing number of Chinese luxury buyers are novices to the luxury world, knowing little about luxury brands.

They usually prefer functional values, such as quality, material, design or craft, to emotional connections of a certain luxury item.

China's young luxury shoppers at this moment are excited about owning a certain number of luxury goods. Not everyone understands the different connotations and history of luxury brands and different lifestyle they represent.

Furthermore, conspicuous consumption serves more or less a permit to enter one or more wealth-measured exclusive clubs for China's new money.

Luxury goods for many Chinese represent a label of social status and wealth. That is to say, if some of your friends who earn about the same salary as you do can buy Louis Vuitton bags, you are inclined to think that you can also afford it and should buy one too.

课文 2　Text B

Section Ⅰ: Dialog

Interpret the following dialog alternatively into English and Chinese.

售货员: Hello, Miss. Can I help you?
顾客: 我非常喜欢这个鼻烟壶。真是一件漂亮的艺术品啊!
售货员: You are right. Look at the inner painting. Wonderful, isn't it?
顾客: 是啊,真是不可思议。我真想知道是怎么画进去的。
售货员: It's a unique art form, native to China.
顾客: 我来之前听说过。对了,这是什么材料的?　玻璃吗?
售货员: No, it's not glass. It's jade.
顾客: 瓶子上有几个字。写的什么?
售货员: Nan de hu tu, meaning ignorance is a rare blessing.
顾客: 有道理。能让我好好看看吗?
售货员: Sure. Here you are.
顾客: 谢谢。你们这儿的鼻烟壶真是品种齐全啊。
售货员: You said it. You name it, we have it.
顾客: 这个多少钱?
售货员: 588 yuan.

顾客：什么？这不是明抢吗？我知道艺术品很贵，也不至于那么贵吧。

售货员：Actually it's not the most expensive one in our shop. Generally speaking, our snuff bottles are good and affordable. You can hardly buy similar ones at such a price elsewhere. You get what you pay for.

顾客：能打个折吗？

售货员：Sorry, no second price.

顾客：如果我买4个，可以打折吗？

售货员：In that case, I'll give you 12% off. And that's the bottom line.

顾客：好吧。要4个。请您给我包好。

售货员：No problem.

Section Ⅱ: Passage
Interpret the following passage into Chinese.

Tourist Economy

Tourism is the travel for recreational, leisure, family or business purposes, usually of a limited duration. Tourism is commonly associated with trans-national travel, but it may also refer to traveling to another location within the same country. The World Tourism Organization defines tourists as people "traveling to and staying in places outside their usual environment for not more than one consecutive year for leisure, business and other purposes".

Tourism has become a popular global leisure activity. Tourism can be domestic or international, and international tourism has both incoming and outgoing implications on a country's balance of payments. Today, tourism is a major source of income for many countries, and affects the economy of both the source and host countries. In some cases, it is of vital importance.

Tourism suffered as a result of a strong economic slowdown between the second half of 2008 and the end of 2009, and the sudden outbreak of the H1N1 influenza virus. It then slowly recovered, with international tourist arrivals surpassing the milestone 1 billion tourists globally for the first time in history in 2012. International tourism receipts grew to US＄1.03 trillion in 2011. In 2012, China became the largest spender in international tourism globally with US＄102 billion, surpassing Germany and United States. China and emerging markets significantly increase their spending over the past decade, with Russia and Brazil as noteworthy examples.

Tourism is an important, even vital, source of income for many countries. Its importance was recognized in the *Manila Declaration on World Tourism of 1980* as "an activity essential to the life of nations because of its direct effects on the social, cultural, educational, and economic sectors of national societies and on their international relations".

Tourism brings in large amounts of income into a local economy in the form of payment for goods and services needed by tourists, accounting for 30% of the world's trade of services, and 6% of overall exports of goods and services. It also creates opportunities for employment in the service sector of the economy associated with tourism.

The service industries which benefit from tourism include transportation services, such as airlines, cruise ships, and taxicabs; hospitality services, such as accommodations, including hotels and resorts; and entertainment venues, such as amusement parks, shopping malls, music venues, and theatres. This is in addition to goods bought by tourists, including souvenirs, clothing and other supplies.

Section Ⅲ: Passage
Interpret the following passage into English.

奢侈品之恋（第二部分）

新贵
中国的奢侈品消费者非常年轻。他们中的许多人要么是个体户，要么是属于日益庞大的中产阶级。其中，80%都是45岁以下的。相比之下，美国和日本的年轻奢侈品消费者仅有30%和19%。

年轻人的这种炫耀性消费是中国经济社会转型的副产品。经济腾飞给中国人带来了日益增长的购买力，而他们还不善于利用。这些年轻的奢侈品买家需要宽容，需要引导，因为奢侈品所带来的情感上的满足将随着经济的持续增长而慢慢消失。

本土化
大品牌越来越意识到中国市场的重要性，都瞄准了中国来缓解危机。

在中国各大都市中心以及二线城市，带有全球公认的名牌标志的精品店正变得越来越明显。

全球奢侈品牌依然依赖在都市中心的旗舰店以及在时尚杂志上做广告来推销其认知度，不过很多品牌已经跨出北京、上海，进军二三线城市。

尽管中国一半的富裕消费者现居住在中国最大的10个城市,但四分之三的新贵在5至7年内将出现在非一线城市,这些人对自己的环境非常熟悉。他们主要是当地的企业家,不大可能随着收入的增加而搬到大城市。

因此,许多知名品牌在中国开设新店。除此之外,这些全球知名品牌在经济低迷时正以优惠的价格处理其库存商品。

为了让更多的中国人买得起他们的产品,为了获得更大的市场份额,高端品牌再出新的举措,推出了带有自己商标的饰物,如领带、袖扣等,或者采取品牌延伸策略,迎合年轻客户的爱好,因为在中国二三线城市没有多少人愿意拿出月薪的一半购买一个路易威登入门包。不过,奢侈品牌正通过向广大的消费群推销物美价廉的饰物建立其品牌认知度。

Section Ⅰ: Dialog

售货员:小姐,您好。您想要点什么?

顾客:I love this snuff bottle. What a beautiful work of art!

售货员:没错。看看这个内画,是不是很了不起?

顾客:You bet. That's simply incredible. I was wondering how they could make it.

售货员:这是一种独特的艺术形式,根儿就在中国。

顾客:I heard of that before I came. By the way, what material is it made of? Is it glass?

售货员:不是玻璃,是玉石。

顾客:There are some characters on it. What are they?

售货员:难得糊涂。

顾客:That makes sense. May I have a close look at it?

售货员:当然,给您。

顾客:Thanks. You do have a large selection of them.

售货员:没错,应有尽有。

顾客:How much is it?

售货员:588元。

顾客:What? It's daylight robbery, isn't it? I know works of art are expensive. But I don't think they should be so expensive.

售货员:实际上,这并不是我们店里最贵的。我们的鼻烟壶一般来说物美价廉。您在别的地方很难以这个价格买到类似的产品了。一分价钱一分货嘛!

顾客：Can you give me a discount then?
售货员：对不起，一口价。
顾客：What if I take 4?
售货员：那样的话，8.8折吧。不能再低了。
顾客：OK, I'll take 4. Could you please pack them well for me?
售货员：没问题。

Section Ⅱ：Passage

旅游经济

旅游就是出行，或娱乐，或休闲，或为了家人，或为了生意。旅游一般都时间不长。说到旅游，人们往往会想到去国外旅行，然而，旅游也可以指到国内的某个地方去旅行。世界旅游组织给游客下的定义是，"到自己熟知环境以外的地方去或者待在自己熟知环境以外的地方的人，连续不超过1年，或为了休闲，或为了业务，或为了其他目的"。

旅游已经成为一个广受欢迎的全球性的休闲活动。旅游可以是国内旅游，也可以是国际旅游。国际旅游，或为入境旅游，或为出境旅游，影响一个国家的国际收支平衡。今天，旅游是许多国家的主要收入来源，既影响输出国的经济，也影响目的国的经济。在某些情况下，这还是至关重要的。

2008年下半年至2009年年底，经济大幅放缓，H1N1流感病毒突然爆发，使得旅游业蒙受打击。后来，慢慢恢复。2012年，全球国际游客数量首次超过10亿，这是一个里程碑的数字。2011年，国际旅游收入达到1.03万亿美元。2012年，中国成为全球国际旅游最大的支出国，总额达到1020亿美元，超过德国和美国。中国和其他新兴市场，在过去10年里，大大增加了其旅游支出，俄罗斯和巴西就是明显的例子。

旅游是许多国家重要的、甚至是至关重要的收入来源。它的重要性在《1980年马尼拉世界旅游宣言》中得到肯定。"旅游，对各民族的生活来说，是一项必不可少的活动，这是因为它对民族国家的社会、文化、教育和经济领域乃至其国际关系产生直接影响。"

旅游为当地经济带来巨大的收入，主要是游客购买所需的商品及服务，占世界服务贸易的30%，占商品及服务整体出口总量的6%。它还为与旅游相关的服务行业创造了就业机会。

受益于旅游业的服务行业包括交通服务（如航空公司、邮轮、出租车等）、酒店服务（如住宿，包括酒店和度假村等）和娱乐场所（如游乐园、购物中心、音乐场馆、剧院等）。这其中还不包括游客所购买的商品，如纪念品、服装和其他用品等。

Section Ⅲ: Passage

A Love Affair with Luxury (Part Two)

New Money

China's luxury shoppers are strikingly young, many of whom are self-employed or part of a growing professional middle class. Eighty percent of them are under 45, compared with 30 percent of luxury shoppers in the United States and 19 percent in Japan.

The popularity of conspicuous consumption among young people is a by-product of China's economic and social transformation where the economic takeoff has given the Chinese growing purchasing power they are not yet adept at using. These young luxury buyers need tolerance as well as guidance because the emotional satisfaction luxury shopping can generate for Chinese consumers will diminish as the economy keeps growing.

Localization

Now more aware of the importance of the Chinese market, major designer brands are looking to China to cushion the crisis.

In the country's various metropolitan hubs as well as second-tier cities, boutique stores carrying the logos of globally recognized brands are becoming increasingly visible.

While global luxury brands continue to rely on their flagship stores in metropolitan hubs and advertisements in fashion magazines for brand recognition, many of them have reached out beyond Beijing and Shanghai in second- and third-tier cities.

Although half of China's wealthy consumers are now living in China's 10 largest cities, three-quarters of new wealthy customers in five to seven years will be those outside of the first-tier cities — people who have close connections with their environment. These are mainly local entrepreneurs who are not likely to move to large cities with an income increase.

As a result, many designer brands opened new stores in China. Apart from that, these globally eminent brands are now offering price discounts to offload their stock amid the economic downturn.

In other moves to make their products affordable for more Chinese and to gain a larger market share, high-end brands are launching more logo-adorned accessories, such as neckties and cuff links, or resorting to brand extension strategy to cater to young customers, for not many in China's second-and third-tier cities are willing to spend half of their monthly income on a basic Louis Vuitton bag, but through sales of accessories affordable to a much larger customer base, luxury brands build up brand recognition.

第7单元
出境入境

Entry and Exit

课文 1　Text A

Section Ⅰ: Dialog
Interpret the following dialog alternatively into English and Chinese.

一、换登机牌 One: At the Check-in Counter

机场人员：Your passport and your ticket, please, sir.
游客：给。
机场人员：Thank you. And how many pieces of luggage do you have?
游客：嗯，一件托运行李、一个旅行箱和一个背包。
机场人员：Are you checking the suitcase, too?
游客：不，我随身带着好了。
机场人员：Good. I'm sorry your bag is over the weight limit by 3 kilos.
游客：超重 3 千克？天哪，那怎么办？
机场人员：You either take some of your items out or pay the...
游客：嗯，知道了。交行李超重费。多少钱？
机场人员：20 dollars per kilo. So it adds up to 60 dollars.
游客：噢，太多了。我还是拿出一些东西来，让朋友带回去。
机场人员：As you please.
游客：让您久等了。现在可以了吗？
机场人员：Perfect, sir. OK, done. Here's your boarding pass, sir. Pay attention to the airport loudspeaker system and board your flight at Gate 4 after the security check.
游客：谢谢。
机场人员：Have a nice flight.

二、过安检 Two: Security Check

海关官员：May I see your passport, please?
游客：这儿呢。
海关官员：Thank you, sir. Do you have anything to declare?
游客：没有，长官。
海关官员：OK, please put your lap-top, iPad, cell phone and all other electronic things in this tray.
游客：好的，长官。

海关官员：Lighters, shampoo, and water are not allowed.

游客：我没带这些，长官。

海关官员：Just a moment. Would you follow me? Open your backpack, please, sir. OK, what's in this box?

游客：豆瓣酱。

海关官员：Sorry, sir. You are not supposed to bring it onto the plane with you. You can either let us take care of it or go back to have it checked in.

游客：那样的话，还是交给你们处理吧。

海关官员：OK. You may go now. Bon voyage.

游客：再见。

Section II: Passage
Interpret the following passage into Chinese.

The Sydney Opera House

The Sydney Opera House is a multi-venue performing arts centre in Sydney, New South Wales, Australia. Situated on Bennelong Point in Sydney Harbour, close to the Sydney Harbour Bridge, the facility is adjacent to the Sydney central business district and the Royal Botanic Gardens, between Sydney and Farm Coves.

Though its name suggests a single venue, the project comprises multiple performance venues which together are among the busiest performing arts centers in the world — hosting over 1,500 performances each year attended by some 1.2 million people. The venues produce and present a wide range of in-house productions and accommodate numerous performing arts companies, including four key resident companies: Opera Australia, The Australian Ballet, the Sydney Theatre Company and the Sydney Symphony Orchestra. As one of the most popular visitor attractions in Australia, more than seven million people visit the site each year, with 300,000 people participating annually in a guided tour of the facility.

The facility, which features a modern expressionist design, was designed by Danish architect Jørn Utzon. Before its competition, Jørn Utzon had won 7 of the 18 competitions he had entered but had never seen any of his designs built. Utzon's submitted concept for the Sydney Opera House was almost universally admired and considered groundbreaking. At first, Utzon worked very successfully with the rest of the design team and the client, but, as the project progressed, the local government insisted on progressive revisions. Besides, they did not fully appreciate the costs or work involved in design and construction. Tensions ensued. In the end, Utzon had no choice but to resign. He left the country never to return.

The Opera House was formally completed in 1973, having cost $102 million. The original cost and scheduling estimates in 1957 projected a cost of $7 million and completion date of January 26, 1963. In actuality, the project was completed 10 years late and more than 14 times over budget.

In the late 1990s, the Sydney Opera House Trust resumed communication with Utzon in an attempt to effect a reconciliation with him and to secure his involvement in future changes to the building. In 1999, he was appointed by the Trust as a design consultant for future work. In 2004, the first interior space rebuilt to an Utzon design was opened, and renamed "The Utzon Room" in his honor. In April 2007, he proposed a major reconstruction of the Opera Theatre.

Identified as one of the 20th century's most distinctive buildings and one of the most famous performing arts centres in the world, the facility is managed by the Sydney Opera House Trust, under the auspices of the New South Wales Ministry of the Arts. It became a UNESCO World Heritage Site on June 28, 2007.

Section Ⅲ: Passage
Interpret the following passage into English.

海 关

海关是一个国家机关,其职责是征收关税,并对出入国境的货物,包括动物、个人物品和危险物品进行监管。移民局往往通过各种名目和安排对出入境人员进行监控。移民局通常检查人员的证件,确保其有资格入境,逮捕那些被国内或国际通缉的犯人,并阻止危险人员入境。

每个国家对进出口商品都有自己的法律法规,由海关负责执行。一些商品的进口或出口可能会受到限制或遭到禁止。

在大多数国家,海关是通过政府间的协议和国际法来征收关税的。所谓关税,指的是对进出口货物课征的一种税收。

尚未通关的商品存放在关税区,通常叫作保税仓库,等候处理。所有获得授权的口岸都是关税区。

在一些国家,海关为抵达许多国际机场和某些公路口岸的入境旅客设立红色通道和绿色通道。需要申报的旅客走红色通道,无须申报的旅客走绿色通道。走绿色通道的旅客会接受现场抽查,这样会节省时间。然而,如果选择绿色通道的旅客所携带的物品超过海关上限或者属于违禁物品，便会因借用绿色通道向海关进行虚假申报而遭到起诉。

欧盟机场内还设有一个蓝色通道。由于欧盟属于一个关税联盟，因此，欧盟国家之间的旅客不需要支付关税。如果货物随后售出，可能会征收增值税和消费税，但这是在货物售出后征收的，不是在海关收取。非欧盟国家旅客走蓝色通道，可能会对他们进行违禁品检查。此外，对从其他欧盟成员国进口的一些烟草和酒类也有限制。如果超出上限，使用蓝色通道也是不合适的。

Section Ⅰ：Dialog

一、换登机牌

机场人员：先生，请出示您的护照和机票。
游客：Here you are.
机场人员：谢谢。您一共有几件行李？
游客：Well, I have a bag, a suitcase and a backpack.
机场人员：您的旅行箱也拖运吗？
游客：No. I'd rather carry it with me.
机场人员：好的。不好意思，您的行李超重3千克。
游客：Over the weight limit by 3 kilos? Oh my, what shall I do then?
机场人员：您可以拿出一些东西来，或者交……
游客：Yes, I know. Excess luggage charge. But how much is it?
机场人员：每千克20美元，一共60美元。
游客：Oh, that's way too much. I'd better take some of my things out and let my friend take them back.
机场人员：随您。
游客：Thanks for waiting. Is it OK now?
机场人员：很好，先生。好，行了。先生，请拿好您的登机牌，注意收听机场广播。通过安检后，请在4号登机口登机。
游客：Thank you.
机场人员：旅途愉快。

二、过安检

海关官员：请出示您的护照。

游客: Here it is.

海关官员：谢谢，先生。您有什么需要申报的吗?

游客：Nothing, Officer.

海关官员：很好。请把笔记本电脑、iPad、手机及其他电子产品放在这个托盘里。

游客：Ok, Officer.

海关官员：禁止携带打火机、洗发香波和水。

游客: No, I don't have them, Officer.

海关官员：等一下。请这边走。先生，请打开您的背包。好的，这个盒子里装的是什么?

游客: Bean sauce.

海关官员：对不起，先生。您不能把这个带上飞机。您可以把它交给我们，也可以回去办理托运。

游客: In that case, I'd better leave it to you.

海关官员: 好的。您可以走了。一路平安。

游客: Bye.

Section II: Passage

悉尼歌剧院

悉尼歌剧院是澳大利亚新南威尔士州悉尼市的一个多场馆表演艺术中心。它位于悉尼港的贝恩朗角，离悉尼港大桥不远，毗邻悉尼中央商务区和皇家植物园，介于悉尼市和农场湾之间。

虽然从名字上看是个单一的地点，然而，该工程是由多个演艺场馆组成的。这些场馆一起成为世界上最繁忙的表演艺术中心之一，每年举办 1500 多场表演，观众达 120 万人。场馆推出各种各样的室内表演，接待形形色色的行为艺术公司，包括 4 家重要的驻馆公司，即澳大利亚歌剧院、澳大利亚芭蕾舞团、悉尼戏剧公司和悉尼交响乐团。作为澳大利亚最受欢迎的旅游景点之一，每年有 700 多万人来到这里，其中 30 万人在导游的陪同下参观歌剧院。

歌剧院的设计风格属于现代表现主义，是由丹麦建筑师约恩·乌松设计的。在项目竣工前，约恩曾参加了 18 个设计大赛，获得 7 个大奖。然而，他的设计只是停留在图纸上。约恩提交的悉尼歌剧院设计理念几乎得到交口赞誉，被认为是开山之作。一开始，约恩和设计团队的成员及客户都合作得很好，但是，随着项目的进展，当地政府要求进行大幅度修改。此外，他们对设计成本、建造成本没有充分的思想准备，随之双方关系变得非常紧张。最后，乌松别无选择，只能辞职。他愤而离去，从此未再踏上澳大利亚的土地。

悉尼歌剧院于1973年正式完工，总共耗资1.02亿美元。1957年，最初的预算成本为700万美元，竣工日期为1963年1月26日。事实上，项目竣工推迟了10年，成本也是原先预算的14倍以上。

20世纪90年代末，悉尼歌剧院托拉斯与乌松取得联系，试图与他达成和解，确保他参与未来的改建工作。1999年，乌松被托拉斯任命为未来设计顾问。2004年，第一个按乌松设计重建的内部空间对外营业，并更名为"乌松厅"，以此向他表示敬意。2007年4月，他提出，要对"歌剧院"进行大规模重建。

悉尼歌剧院被公认为20世纪最独特的建筑和最著名的表演艺术中心之一。剧院由新南威尔士艺术部旗下的悉尼歌剧院托拉斯负责管理。2007年6月28日，成为联合国教科文组织世界遗产。

Section Ⅲ: Passage

Customs

Customs is an authority or agency in a country responsible for collecting customs duties and for controlling the flow of goods, including animals, personal effects, and hazardous items, into and out of a country. The movement of people into and out of a country is normally monitored by immigration authorities, under a variety of names and arrangements. The immigration authorities normally check for appropriate documentation, verify that a person is entitled to enter the country, apprehend people wanted by domestic or international arrest warrants, and impede the entry of people deemed dangerous to the country.

Each country has its own laws and regulations for the import and export of goods into and out of a country, which its customs authority enforces. The import or export of some goods may be restricted or forbidden.

In most countries, customs are attained through government agreements and international laws. A customs duty is a tariff or tax on the importation or exportation of goods.

Commercial goods not yet cleared through customs are held in a customs area, often called a bonded store, until processed. All authorized ports are recognized customs areas.

In some countries, customs procedures for arriving passengers at many international airports and some road crossings are separated into red and green channels. Passengers with goods to declare go through the red channel. Passengers with nothing to declare go through the green channel. These passengers are subject only to spot checks and save time. However, if a passenger going through the green channel is found to be carrying goods above the customs limits or prohibited items, he or she may be prosecuted for making a false declaration to customs, by virtue of having gone through the green channel.

Airports within the European Union also have a blue channel. As the EU is a customs union, travelers between EU countries do not have to pay customs duties. Value-added tax and excise duties may be applicable if the goods are subsequently sold, but these are collected when the goods are sold, not at the border. Passengers arriving from other EU countries go through the blue channel, where they may still be subject to checks for prohibited or restricted goods. In addition, limitations exist on various tobacco and alcohol products being imported from other EU member states, and if those limitations are being exceeded, use of the blue channel would be inappropriate.

课文 2　Text B

Section Ⅰ: Dialog
Interpret the following dialog alternatively into English and Chinese.

一、在飞机上 One: On the Plane

空乘人员：Welcome aboard, sir. You are one of our last passengers today. May I help you find your seat?

游客：好的，请。这是我的登机牌。

空乘人员：So you are flying economy class. Your seat is in the middle of the cabin. Follow me, please.

游客：好的，谢谢。

空乘人员：A window seat on the right side. Here you are, sir.

游客：多谢。我可以把行李箱放这儿吗？

空乘人员：You'd better put it in the overhead rack, sir, because it will be a long flight.

游客：好的，没问题。

空乘人员：Enjoy your flight, sir.

游客：谢谢。对了，小姐，飞机上有什么喝的？

空乘人员：We have juice, coffee, coke, tea, and beer. What would you like to have, sir?

游客：橙汁。

空乘人员：OK. I'll bring it to you right away.

游客：好的。

空乘人员：Here's your juice, sir. Anything else I can do for you?

游客：嗯，请给我拿个枕头、拿条毯子来，恐怕夜间飞行会冷。

空乘人员：You will have them in no time. Is that all, sir?

游客：是的，小姐。谢谢。

空乘人员：OK. Ladies and gentlemen, we are ready to take off. Please turn off your cell phones and other electronic devices. Make sure you have fastened your seat belt and folded up the small table in front of you. Thanks for flying with us. Enjoy.

二、在入境处 Two: At the Immigration Counter

入境官员：Welcome to America. Your passport, please, miss.

游客：给。

入境官员：Thank you. May I know the purpose of your visit?

游客：观光。

入境官员：Is it a DIY tour or a package tour?

游客：跟团，先生。

入境官员：OK. How long are you going to stay in America?

游客：15天。

入境官员：That's a long time, huh? You are lucky.

游客：是的。

入境官员：Do you have a return ticket to China?

游客：有的，先生。在这儿呢。

入境官员：Thank you. And how much cash are you carrying?

游客：2200美元。

入境官员：Is that all?

游客：嗯，我身上还有一些人民币，2000元左右。

入境官员：So, altogether you have about 2,500 dollars with you.

游客：没错。

入境官员：How are you going to use the money?

游客：旅游。

入境官员：Good. Please fill out this form here.

游客：好的。给。

入境官员：Thank you. And have a nice stay here.

Section Ⅱ: Passage
Interpret the following passage into Chinese.

The Eiffel Tower

The Eiffel Tower is an iron lattice tower located on the Champ de Mars in Paris. It was named after the engineer Gustave Eiffel, whose company designed and built the tower. Erected in 1889 as the entrance arch to the 1889 World's Fair, it was initially criticized by some of France's leading artists and intellectuals for its design, but has become both a global cultural icon of France and one of the most recognizable structures in the world. The tower is the tallest structure in Paris and the most-visited paid monument in the world. The tower received its 250 millionth visitor in 2010.

The tower is 324 meters tall, about the same height as an 81-storey building. During its construction, the Eiffel Tower surpassed the Washington Monument to assume the title of the tallest man-made structure in the world, a title it held for 41 years, until the Chrysler Building in New York City was built in 1930. Because of the addition of the antenna atop the Eiffel Tower in 1957, it is now taller than the Chrysler Building by 5.2 meters. Not including broadcast antennae, it is the second tallest structure in France.

The tower has three levels for visitors, with restaurants on the first and second. The third level observatory's upper platform is 276 meters above the ground, the highest accessible to the public in the European Union. Tickets can be purchased to ascend by stairs or elevator to the first and second levels. The climb from ground level to the first level is over 300 steps. Although there are stairs to the third and highest level, these are usually closed to the public and it is generally only accessible by elevator.

The main structural work was completed at the end of March 1889, and on the 31st, Eiffel celebrated this by leading a group of government officials, accompanied by representatives of the press, to the top of the tower. Since the elevators were not yet in operation, the ascent was made by foot, and took over an hour. Most of the party chose to stop at the lower levels, but only a few completed the climb. The tower was an immediate success with the public, and nearly 30,000 visitors made the 1,710-step climb to the top using the stairs before the elevators entered service on 26 May.

After dark, the tower was lit by hundreds of gas lamps and a beacon sending out three beams of red, white and blue light. Two searchlights were mounted on a circular rail, and were used to illuminate various features of the Exposition. The opening and closing of the Exposition were announced every day by a cannon fired from the top.

Section Ⅲ: Passage
Interpret the following passage into English.

机场安检

机场安检是指利用技术和方法保护旅客、机场工作人员和使用机场的飞机免受偶然的或恶意的伤害，使其远离犯罪和其他威胁。

每天都有大量的人员要进出机场，这使其成为恐怖主义和其他犯罪的潜在目标，这是因为很多人聚集在某个特定地方的缘故。同样，大型客机上的人数较多，袭击飞机会带来大量死亡，一架劫持来的飞机可以用作致命武器，这一切都为恐怖主义提供了一个诱人的目标。

机场安检试图阻止任何威胁或潜在的危险情况产生或进入该国。如果机场安检成功地做到了这一点，那么，危险情况、非法物品或威胁进入飞机、国家或机场的机会就会大大减少。因此，机场安检的目的是保护机场和国家不受任何威胁，让旅客感到自己是安全的，保护国家和人民。

换句话说，航空安全的目的是防止飞机、乘客和机组人员受到伤害，支持国家安全和反恐政策。

20世纪70年代以前，美国机场防止劫机事件发生的安全措施级别很低。20世纪60年代末，在发生了几次备受瞩目的劫机事件之后，美国才出台了一些措施。

1970年，出现了空中便衣警察。但是，人数不多，不足以保护每一个航班。所以，劫机事件继续发生。1972年11月10日劫机事件的直接结果是，美国联邦航空管理局要求所有航空公司从1973年1月5日开始筛查乘客和他们的随身行李。

"9·11"恐怖袭击促使出台更加严格的规定，如限制乘客随身携带行李的数量和种类、要求对那些未能出示政府颁发的带照片的证件的乘客进行严格筛查。

航空运输安全法案要求，自2002年11月19日起，所有乘客筛查必须由联邦雇员进行。因此，旅客和行李筛查现在由国土安全部附属的运输安全管理局负责。

由于增加了安全筛查，一些机场出现了长长的队伍等待安检。为了缓解这个问题，机场为头等舱或商务舱的乘客、某一航班"常客回馈计划"的精英成员推出了"优先通道"。

现在，美国某些机场还使用SPOT技术，即对旅客外表举止特征进行分析的技术。

参考答案

Section Ⅰ： Dialog

一、在飞机上

空乘人员：先生，欢迎乘坐本次航班。您是我们今天这个航班最后几位乘客之一了。让我来帮您找座位吧。

游客：Yes, please. Here's my boarding pass.

空乘人员：哦，您是经济舱。您的座位在机舱中部。请跟我来。

游客：OK, thanks.

空乘人员：右首靠窗户的座位。先生，这是您的座位。

游客：Thank you very much. Can I put my suitcase here?

空乘人员：先生，您最好把它放在头顶上的行李架里，因为是长途飞行。

游客：OK. No problem.

空乘人员：先生，旅途愉快。

游客：Thank you. By the way, what kind of drinks do you have, miss?

空乘人员：有果汁、咖啡、可乐、茶，还有啤酒。先生，您想来点什么？

游客：Orange juice, please.

空乘人员：好的。马上送来。

游客：OK.

空乘人员：先生，这是您要的橙汁。还需要别的吗？

游客：Well, can I have a pillow and a blanket, please? I'm afraid it might be cold during our night flight.

空乘人员：马上就到。先生，就这些吗？

游客：Yes, miss. Thank you.

空乘人员：好的。女士们、先生们，飞机就要起飞了。请关闭您的手机及其他电子设备。系好安全带，收起面前的小桌。感谢大家乘坐我们的航班。旅途愉快。

二、在入境处

入境官员：欢迎到美国来。小姐，请出示您的护照。

游客：Here you are.

入境官员：谢谢。请问，您此行的目的是什么？

游客：I'm here for sightseeing.

入境官员：是自助游，还是跟团？

游客：A package tour, sir.

入境官员：好的。您在美国待多久？

游客：For 15 days.

入境官员：时间不短嘛。您真幸运。

游客：Sure.

入境官员：您有回中国的机票吗？

游客：Yes, sir. Here it is.

入境官员：谢谢。您身上带了多少现金？

游客：I'm carrying 2,200 dollars.

入境官员：就这么多吗？

游客：Well, I also have some Chinese yuan about me. About 2000 yuan.

入境官员：也就是说，一共大约2500美元。

游客：Exactly.

入境官员：您打算怎么用这些钱？

游客：For travelling.

入境官员：很好。请填写一下这张表格。

游客：OK. Here you are.

入境官员：谢谢。祝您在美国生活愉快。

| Section Ⅱ：Passage

埃菲尔铁塔

埃菲尔铁塔是一座镂空结构铁塔，位于巴黎的战神广场。埃菲尔铁塔得名于它的工程师古斯塔夫·埃菲尔，他的公司设计并建造了这座塔。该塔建于1889年，是通往1889年世界博览会的入口拱门。一开始，其设计受到法国一些著名艺术家和学者的抨击，后来却成为法国全球文化的象征，也是世界上最容易辨认的建筑之一。埃菲尔铁塔是巴黎最高的建筑物，也是世界上访问量最大的付费纪念碑。2010年，埃菲尔铁塔迎来了其第2.5亿名参观者。

塔高324米，差不多有81层大楼高。在其建设当中，埃菲尔铁塔就已经超过了华盛顿纪念碑，成为世界上最高的人造建筑物。这个称号持续了41年，直到1930年纽约克莱斯勒大厦的竣工。埃菲尔铁塔1957年在顶部安装了天线，因此，它现在比克莱斯勒大厦高5.2米。不包括广播天线在内，它是法国第二高建筑物。

埃菲尔铁塔分三层，一层和二层都有餐厅。第三层瞭望台离地面276米，是对公众开放的欧盟最高点。买票后，通过楼梯或乘坐电梯，可以登上第一层或第二层。从地面到第一层有300多个台阶。虽然有楼梯通往第三层或最高层，但通常不对游人开放，一般只能乘坐电梯上去。

1889年3月底,埃菲尔铁塔的主体工程竣工。为了庆祝,31日,埃菲尔领着一群政府官员,在媒体代表的陪伴下,登上了塔顶。由于电梯还没有正式运营,一直是走上去的,先后花了一个多小时的时间。大部分人选择留在了一层或二层,只有少数完成了攀登。埃菲尔铁塔一夜成名,在5月26日电梯正式运转之前,近3万名游客完成了1710级台阶的徒步攀登。

夜幕降临,数以百计的煤气灯把埃菲尔铁塔照亮,一座灯塔发出红、白、蓝三束光。两个探照灯安装在一个环形杆上,把世博会的现场照得灯火通明。埃菲尔铁塔顶部早晚各1次炮声宣告每天世博会的开始与结束。

Section Ⅲ: Passage

Airport Security

Airport security refers to the techniques and methods used in protecting passengers, staff and aircraft which use the airports from accidental or malicious harm, crime and other threats.

Large numbers of people pass through airports every day. This presents potential targets for terrorism and other forms of crime because of the number of people located in a particular location. Similarly, the high concentration of people on large airliners, the potential high death rate with attacks on aircraft, and the ability to use a hijacked airplane as a lethal weapon may provide an alluring target for terrorism.

Airport security attempts to prevent any threats or potentially dangerous situations from arising or entering the country. If airport security does succeed in this, then the chances of any dangerous situations, illegal items or threats entering into aircraft, country or airport are greatly reduced. As such, airport security serves several purposes: To protect the airport and country from any threatening events, to reassure the traveling public that they are safe and to protect the country and their people.

In other words, the goal of aviation security is to prevent harm to aircraft, passengers, and crew, as well as support national security and counter-terrorism policy.

Prior to the 1970s American airports had minimal security arrangements to prevent aircraft hijackings. Measures were introduced starting in the late 1960s after several high-profile hijackings.

Sky marshals were introduced in 1970, but there were insufficient numbers to protect every flight, and hijackings continued to take place. As a direct response to the hijacking that happened on November 10, 1972, the Federal Aviation Administration required that all airlines begin screening passengers and their carry-on baggage by January 5, 1973.

The September 11 attacks prompted even tougher regulations, such as limiting the number of and types of items passengers could carry on board aircraft and requiring increased screening for passengers who fail to present a government issued photo ID.

The Aviation and Transportation Security Act required that by November 19, 2002 all passenger screening must be conducted by Federal employees. As a result, passenger and baggage screening is now provided by the Transportation Security Administration, part of the Department of Homeland Security.

With the increase in security screening, some airports saw long queues for security checks. To alleviate this, airports created Premium lines for passengers traveling in First or Business Class, or those who were elite members of a particular airline's Frequent Flyer program.

The "screening passengers by observation techniques" (SPOT) program is operating at some U.S. airports.

第8单元
邮政服务

At the Post Office

课文 1　Text A

Section I: Dialog

Interpret the following dialog alternatively into English and Chinese.

邮局职员：Good afternoon, sir. Can I help you?
顾客：我想寄封信到洛杉矶。
邮局职员：How would you like to send it, sir? By surface mail or airmail?
顾客：平信需要多长时间?
邮局职员：About 15 days, sir.
顾客：航空邮寄呢?
邮局职员：Three to four days, sir.
顾客：那就航空邮寄吧。这是信。
邮局职员：A heavy one, huh? Is there anything else in the envelope?
顾客：就是在这儿拍的一些照片。
邮局职员：In that case, I have to weigh it.
顾客：称吧。
邮局职员：Sorry, sir, your letter is 10 grams overweight. You have to pay extra.
顾客：没关系。邮费是多少?
邮局职员：Altogether it's 7 yuan 80.
顾客：给。
邮局职员：Thanks. But you have forgotten the return address, sir.
顾客：不好意思，我马上就写。
邮局职员：Be sure to include the zip code.
顾客：谢谢，我会的。给您。对了，您觉得我能赶上今天最后一趟邮班吗?
邮局职员：You sure can. The last mail goes out at 5. And here's your change, sir.
顾客：多谢。
邮局职员：You're welcome, sir.

Section II: Passage

Interpret the following passage into Chinese.

Mini-Europe

If stay just one day in Europe, and if you want to visit only one place, make it Mini-Europe. It is the only park where you can have a whistle-stop tour around Europe in a few short hours. A truly unique voyage! You can stroll amid the typical ambiance of the most beautiful towns of the Old Continent.

Mini-Europe is a miniature park located at the foot of the Atomium in Brussels, Belgium. The idea isn't really new, but in Brussels, the capital of the European Union, a Mini-Europe is very appropriate. There are not necessarily the biggest sights in Europe, which are presented, but rather buildings, which show the cultural inheritance of Europe and its manifoldedness. All of the buildings were constructed minutely in a scale of 1 : 25 so that you can get an approximate perception of their real size, when you compare those known buildings to each other. Between the buildings a little "nature" is kept. An artificial canal irrigates the area and supplies the "surroundings" for buildings which are situated at some kind of water. Miniature trains go between different cities, toy cars and boats show the traffic on streets and waterways. Sometimes there are even mini-tourists, admiring the sights. A guide gives the details on all the monuments. At the end of the visit, the "Spirit of Europe" exhibition gives an interactive overview of the European Union in the form of multimedia games.

Roughly 80 cities and 350 buildings are represented. The models cost as much as 350,000 to make.

The park is built on an area of 24,000 m^2. The initial investment was of 10 million in 1989, on its inauguration by Prince Philip of Belgium.

The monuments, many of which were financed by European countries or regions, were chosen for the quality of their architecture or their European symbolism. Most of the monuments were made using moulds. The final copy used to be cast from epoxy resin, but now polyester is used. Three of the monuments were made out of stone (e. g. the tower of Pisa, in marble). A computer-assisted milling procedure was used for two of the models.

After painting the monument was installed on site, together with decorations and lighting. The Cathedral of Santiago de Compostela required more than 24,000 hours of work.

Ground cover plants, dwarf trees, bonsais and grafted trees are used alongside miniature monuments, and the paths are adorned with bushes and flowers.

What is worth mentioning is that, although it is called Mini Europe, it doesn't mean that every European country is represented there. Norway and Iceland are not part of Mini Europe. Neither is Switzerland. This is because those countries are not members of the EU.

All in all, with 350,000 visitors per year and a turnover of 4 million euros, Mini Europe has become one of Brussels' leading attractions.

So, Mini Europe is an absolute must!

Section Ⅲ: Passage
Interpret the following passage into English.

文化旅游

文化旅游是旅游业的一个小类，它关心的是一个国家或地区的文化，尤其是生活在那些地区的人们的生活方式、历史、艺术、建筑、宗教和促进其生活方式形成的其他因素。文化旅游包括城市旅游（尤其是历史名城或大都市）及其文化设施，如博物馆和剧院等。文化旅游也包括乡村旅游，主要展示土著文化社区的传统（如节日、仪式）以及当地人的价值观念和生活方式。人们普遍认为，文化游客的消费大大超过普通游客。这种形式的旅游在世界各地也变得越来越受欢迎。近来，"经合组织"的一份报告突出强调了文化旅游在世界不同角落区域发展中的作用。

一种类型的文化旅游就是参观自己文化之外的任何文化，比如去国外旅行。其他目的地还包括历史遗迹、现代都市区、城镇中的"民族聚居区"、展销会、节日、主题公园和自然生态系统。有证据表明，文化景点和文化活动对游客有着特殊的吸引力。

另一种类型的文化旅游是文学旅游，它关心的是小说中的地点、书中描写的事情以及作者的生活。这可能包括追寻书中人物的足迹、访问与小说或小说家有关的特定地点、参观某一个诗人的坟墓等。一些学者认为，文学旅游是现代的一种世俗朝圣。还有一些与作家有关的路线，需要长途步行，如托马斯·哈代步行道等。

文学游客特别感兴趣的是某些地方如何影响了作家的创作以及作品如何"造就"了某些地方。要想成为一名文学游客，你只需要喜欢书籍、只需要有一颗好奇心就够了。不过，现在有文学指南、文学地图和文学考察可以帮助你。也有许多与作家有关的博物馆，这些博物馆通常设在与作家的出生地和文学生涯有关的建筑物内。

书店旅游也是一种文化旅游。作为一个团体旅游目的地，能够促进非连锁书店的发展。起初，这是一种民间活动，目的是支持当地的书店，因为其中有很多难以与大型连锁书店和网上零售书店一争高下。

提倡书店旅游的人士鼓励学校、图书馆、阅读小组和其他各种机构到非连锁书店比较集中的城镇进行"一日游"或"文学游"。美国各地大小不一的团体常常通过包车组织这样的旅游，其中包括签名售书、作家故乡游、参观历史遗迹等。他们还鼓励当地书店把书店旅游作为经济发展的工具，吸引藏书爱好者到社区。从中受益的还包括当地零售商、餐馆、公交公司和旅游从业人士。这种做法也为各种机构提供了一个外展服务的机会，支持阅读和识字活动。

参考答案

Section Ⅰ：Dialog

邮局职员：先生，下午好。您办理什么业务？
顾客：Yes, I'd like to send a letter to Los Angeles.
邮局职员：先生，您打算怎么邮寄？ 是寄平信呢，还是寄航空信？
顾客：How long will it take to get there by surface mail?
邮局职员：大约15天，先生。
顾客：And by airmail?
邮局职员：3~4天，先生。
顾客：By airmail then. Here's the letter.
邮局职员：挺沉的啊？ 里面还装有什么？
顾客：Just some photos taken here.
邮局职员：那样的话，得称重了。
顾客：Go ahead then.
邮局职员：对不起，先生，您的信超重10克，得额外付邮费。
顾客：It doesn't matter. What is the postage?
邮局职员：一共7元8角。
顾客：Here you are.
邮局职员：谢谢。可是，先生，您忘写寄信人地址了。
顾客：Sorry. I'll do it right away.
邮局职员：别忘了邮政编码。
顾客：Thanks, I will. Here you are. By the way, do you think I can catch the last post today?
邮局职员：当然可以。最后一趟邮班是5点。先生，这是找您的找零头。
顾客：Thank you very much.
邮局职员：不客气，先生。

Section Ⅱ：Passage

迷你欧洲

如果你在欧洲只待1天，如果你只想去一个地方，那么就去迷你欧洲吧。这是唯一花上短短的几个小时就可以转遍欧洲的公园。这是一次非常特殊的旅行！你可以在充满旧大陆情调的美丽城镇里悠闲漫步。

迷你欧洲是一个微型公园，坐落在比利时布鲁塞尔的原子塔下面。这并非什么新奇的想法。不过，在欧盟的总部所在地布鲁塞尔建造一个迷你欧洲确实是一个合适的主意。公园里见到的不一定是欧洲最大的景点，而是可以展示欧洲的文化遗产及其多样面貌的建筑物。所有建筑都是按照1∶25的比例建造的，非常精确。这样，当你把园内建筑跟真实建筑进行比较时，你就会对其真正大小有一个非常接近的概念。建筑物之间，可以看到一个迷你大自然。一条人工运河给公园提供水源，为水边的建筑营造一个"环境"。微型火车在城市间穿梭，玩具汽车、玩具船代表着街道和水路交通。有时，甚至有迷你游客欣赏风景。导游详细介绍园内的纪念碑。在参观的最后，"欧洲风采展"以互动多媒体游戏的方式把欧盟展现在游人面前。

园内大约有80个城市和350个代表建筑。模型的成本高达35万欧元。

公园建在2.4万平方米的土地上。1989年，比利时的菲利普亲王亲自揭幕，初始投资为1000万欧元。

这些具有纪念意义的建筑大都是由欧洲国家或地区出资建成的。入选标准要么是因为其建筑质量好，要么是因为它是欧洲的象征。其中，大多数都是用模具制成的。最后的成品过去是用环氧树脂制成的，但现在用的是聚酯纤维。其中3座建筑是用石头制成的，如比萨斜塔就是用大理石制成的，2个模型采用的是机助粉磨工艺。

粉刷完毕后，建筑物在现场安装，同时配上装饰和照明。圣地亚哥大教堂耗费了2.4万多个小时才安装完毕。

迷你建筑旁边有地被植物、矮树、盆景和嫁接植物，灌木和花卉装饰着小径。

值得一提的是，尽管叫作迷你欧洲，但并不意味着每一个欧洲国家的建筑在园内都能找到。挪威和冰岛就不是迷你欧洲的一部分，瑞士也不是，这是因为这些国家并不是欧盟成员。

总之，迷你欧洲每年的游客人数高达35万，营业额400万欧元，已经成为布鲁塞尔的主要景点之一。

因此，迷你欧洲是你的必去之地！

Section Ⅲ: Passage

Cultural Tourism

Cultural tourism is the subset of tourism concerned with a country or region's culture, specifically the lifestyle of the people in those geographical areas, the history of those people, their art, architecture, religion(s), and other elements that helped shape their way of life. Cultural tourism includes tourism in urban areas, particularly historic or large cities and their cultural facilities such as museums and theatres. It can also include tourism in rural areas showcasing the traditions of indigenous cultural communities (i.e. festivals, rituals), and their values and lifestyle. It is generally agreed that cultural tourists spend substantially more than standard tourists do. This form of tourism is also becoming generally more popular throughout the world, and a recent OECD report has highlighted the role that cultural tourism can play in regional development in different world regions.

One type of cultural tourism is visiting any culture other than one's own such as traveling to a foreign country. Other destinations include historical sites, modern urban districts, "ethnic pockets" of towns, fairs and festivals, theme parks and natural ecosystems. It has been shown that cultural attractions and events are particularly strong magnets for tourism.

Another type of cultural tourism is literary tourism that deals with places and events from fictional texts as well as the lives of their authors. This could include following the route taken by a fictional character, visiting particular place associated with a novel or a novelist, or visiting a poet's grave. Some scholars regard literary tourism as a contemporary type of secular pilgrimage. There are also long-distance walking routes associated with writers, such as the Thomas Hardy Way.

Literary tourists are specifically interested in how places have influenced writing and at the same time how writing has created places. In order to become a literary tourist you need only book-love and an inquisitive mindset; however, there are literary guides, literary maps, and literary tours to help you on your way. There are also many museums associated with writers, and these are usually housed in buildings associated with a writer's birth or literary career.

Bookstore tourism is also a type of cultural tourism that promotes independent bookstores as a group travel destination. It started as a grassroots effort to support locally owned and operated bookshops, many of which have struggled to compete with large bookstore chains and online retailers.

Those who promote bookstore tourism encourage schools, libraries, reading groups and other miscellaneous organizations to create day-trips and literary outings to cities and towns with a concentration of independent bookstores. Groups of various sizes around the U.S. have offered such excursions, usually via a chartered bus, and often incorporating book signings, author home tours and historical sites. They also encourage local booksellers to attract bibliophiles to their communities by employing bookstore tourism as an economic development tool. Others benefiting include local retailers, restaurants, bus companies and travel professionals. The effort also provides organizations with an outreach opportunity to support reading and literacy.

课文 2 Text B

顾客: Hello. I'd like to send this package to France by parcel post.
邮局职员: 好的。小姐,里面装的是什么?
顾客: T-shirts and souvenirs.
邮局职员: 航空邮寄,还是普通邮寄?
顾客: By EMS, please.
邮局职员: 请填写这张表格。写上您的姓名、地址以及邮寄的东西。
顾客: OK. Here you are. Is it OK?
邮局职员: 嗯,您知道收件人的手机号码吗?
顾客: Yes.
邮局职员: 也写下来。您要是有电子信箱也写上。
顾客: OK.
邮局职员: 您要上保险吗?
顾客: Yes, I do. Insure it for 50 euros, please.
邮局职员: 50 欧元,也就是 …… 365 元 3 角 6 分。
顾客: Yes. What is the postage then?
邮局职员: 您的包裹重 5.5 千克。每千克 16 元,一共是 88 元。
顾客: What if the package is lost?
邮局职员: 不会的,小姐。
顾客: I mean if.
邮局职员: 嗯,如果丢失了,我们会按国际邮寄惯例进行赔偿。也就是说,最多 830 元。
顾客: I see. I know you have a very good reputation. I know this won't happen. I was just asking. Sorry.
邮局职员: 没事,小姐,您有权利过问。
顾客: OK. Here's 100 yuan.
邮局职员: 这是找您的零头和收据。
顾客: Thank you. Goodbye.
邮局职员: 再见。

Section Ⅱ: Passage
Interpret the following passage into Chinese.

Yellowstone National Park

Yellowstone National Park is, as its name suggests, a national park located primarily in the U.S. state of Wyoming, although it also extends into Montana and Idaho. Widely held to be the first national park in the world, Yellowstone is known for its wildlife and its many geothermal features, especially Old Faithful Geyser, one of the most popular features in the park. It has many types of ecosystems, but the subalpine forest is most abundant. It is part of the South Central Rockies forests eco-region.

Native Americans have lived in the Yellowstone region for at least 11,000 years. The region was bypassed during the Lewis and Clark Expedition in the early 19th century. Aside from visits by mountain men during the early-to-mid-19th century, organized exploration did not begin until the late 1860s. The U.S. Army was commissioned to oversee the park just after its establishment. In 1917, administration of the park was transferred to the national Park Service, which had been created the previous year. Hundreds of structures have been built and are protected for their architectural and historical significance, and researchers have examined more than 1,000 archaeological sites.

Yellowstone National Park spans an area of 3,468.4 square miles (8,983 km^2), comprising lakes, canyons, rivers and mountain ranges. Yellowstone Lake is one of the largest high-altitude lakes in North America and is centered over the Yellowstone Caldera, the largest super-volcano on the continent. The Caldera is considered an active volcano. It has erupted with tremendous force several times in the last two million years. Half of the world's geothermal features are in Yellowstone, fueled by this ongoing volcanism. Lava flows and rocks from volcanic eruptions cover most of the land area of Yellowstone. The park is the centerpiece of the Greater Yellowstone Ecosystem, the largest remaining nearly-intact ecosystem in the Earth's northern temperate zone.

Hundreds of species of mammals, birds, fish and reptiles have been documented, including several that are either endangered or threatened. The vast forests and grasslands also include unique species of plants. Yellowstone Park is the largest and most famous megafauna location in the Continental United States. Grizzly bears, wolves, and free-ranging herds of bisons and elks live in the park. The Yellowstone Park bison herd is the oldest and largest public bison herd in the United States. Forest fires occur in the park each year; in the large forest fires of 1988, nearly one third of the park was burnt. Yellowstone has numerous recreational opportunities, including hiking, camping, boating, fishing and sight-seeing. Paved roads provide close access to the major geothermal areas as well as some of the lakes and waterfalls. During the winter, visitors often access the park by way of guided tours that use either snow coaches or snowmobiles.

Section Ⅲ: Passage
Interpret the following passage into English.

田园旅游

田园旅游，从广义的角度来说，包括把游客带到农场或牧场的以农业为基础的任何活动。田园旅游在世界不同的地方有着不同的定义，比如在意大利，有时特指在农场小住。在其他地方，田园旅游包括各种各样的活动，如在农产品摊位直接购买农产品、穿越玉米迷宫、采摘水果、喂动物，或在农场留宿。

田园旅游是一种"利基旅游"，在包括澳大利亚、加拿大、美国等世界许多地方都被认为是一个增长行业。拿美国来说，田园旅游在美国非常普遍。田园游客有很多活动可以选择，包括采摘水果蔬菜、骑马、品尝蜂蜜、了解葡萄酒知识及奶酪制作工艺，或在农场礼品商店和农场摊位购买当地和地区特色农产品或手工制作的礼品。

根据美国农业部州际研究、教育和推广局的报告，"旅游对美国的经济越来越重要。堪萨斯联邦储备委员会基于 2000 年的数据进行的保守估计表明，旅行和旅游业为全美就业率贡献了 3.6 个百分点。更能说明问题的数据来自美国旅游业协会。该数据表明，美国每 18 个人当中就有 1 人的工作直接来自旅游支出。"

根据加州大学的"小农场中心"的看法，"农业旅游或田园旅游，是小型农场和农村社区提高收入和潜在经济活力的一个选择。某些形式的田园旅游产业在加州发展得很好，如展会、节日等"。加州大学的"小农场中心"开发了一个加州田园旅游数据库，"为游客和潜在的企业家提供加州现有的田园旅游目的地信息"。

人们对食品生产越来越感兴趣。他们想亲眼见见农民和加工人员，与他们聊聊食品生产的过程。对于许多参观农场的人（尤其是孩子）来说，造访农场标志着他们第一次亲眼目睹食物的来源，不管是奶牛、生长在地里的玉米，还是从树上摘下来的苹果。所以，对儿童也好，对成人也罢，田园旅游结果都是一次集放松、休息和教育于一体的旅游。

参考答案

Section I : Dialog

顾客：您好。我想把这个包裹寄往法国。

邮局职员：Sure. What's in it, miss?

顾客：T恤衫和纪念品。

邮局职员：Would you like to send it by airmail or ordinary mail?

顾客：特快专递。

邮局职员：Fill out this form, please. Put down your name, address, and contents.

顾客：好的。给。这样行吗？

邮局职员：Well, do you know the cell phone number of the addressee?

顾客：知道。

邮局职员：Put that down, too. And your email account also if you have one.

顾客：好的。

邮局职员：Do you want to insure it?

顾客：是的。保50欧元。

邮局职员：Fifty euros. That equals...365 yuan 36.

顾客：是的。邮费是多少？

邮局职员：Your package is 5.5 kilos. The postage is 16 yuan per kilo. So yours is 88 yuan.

顾客：要是包裹丢了怎么办？

邮局职员：I don't think it will happen, miss.

顾客：我是说"要是"。

邮局职员：Well, if it is lost, we will compensate for your loss in line with international mailing practices. That is to say, you can get 830 yuan at most.

顾客：明白了。我知道你们的名声很好。我知道不会发生。我只是随便问问，不好意思。

邮局职员：It's all right, miss. You have the right to ask.

顾客：好的。这是100元。

邮局职员：Here's your change and your receipt.

顾客：谢谢。再见。

邮局职员：Bye.

Section Ⅱ：Passage

黄石国家公园

黄石国家公园，顾名思义，是一个国家级公园，主要位于美国怀俄明州，当然，它还延伸到蒙大拿州和爱达荷州。黄石国家公园是公认的世界上第一个国家公园，因野生动物及诸多地热特征而闻名。特别是"老守信"喷泉，它是公园里最受欢迎的景点之一。黄石国家公园有很多类型的生态系统，但这里最多的要属亚高山森林，它是落基山脉中南部森林生态区的一部分。

印第安人在黄石地区生活了至少11000年。19世纪初，刘易斯和克拉克探险队从这里绕过。19世纪初期至中期，只有山民到过此地。有组织的探险直到19世纪60年代末才开始进行。公园成立后，委托美国陆军代管。1917年，公园的管理权转移到1916年刚刚成立的国家公园管理局手里。数百种建筑拔地而起，并因其建筑风格和历史意义得到保护。研究人员考察过1000多个考古遗址。

黄石国家公园占地面积3468.4平方英里（8983平方千米），包括湖泊、峡谷、河流和山脉。黄石湖是北美海拔最高的大湖之一，是北美最大的超级火山黄石火山口的中心。黄石火山是一座活火山，在过去200万年里爆发过数次，且威力巨大。世界上一半的地热特征在黄石，主要是因为火山在持续活动。火山喷发出来的熔岩流和岩石覆盖了黄石公园的大部分土地。公园是大黄石生态系统的中心，是地球北温带仅存的、最大的、保存最好的生态系统。

数百种哺乳动物、鸟类、鱼类和爬行动物已登记在册，包括一些存在生存危机的或者处于濒危行列的物种。巨大的森林中和广袤的草地上也生长着一些独特的植物。黄石公园拥有美国大陆上最著名的巨型动物。灰熊、狼以及自由觅食的野牛群和麋鹿群都在公园里生活着。黄石公园内的美洲野牛群是美国历史最长、规模最大的公共野牛群。该公园每年都会发生森林火灾；在1988年的特大森林火灾中，几乎三分之一的公园被烧毁。黄石公园有许多娱乐机会，包括徒步旅行、露营、划船、钓鱼和观光等。铺好的道路让人轻而易举地到达主要地热区域、湖泊和瀑布。冬天，游客们经常乘坐雪地车或者雪橇在导游的陪同下前往公园游览。

Section Ⅲ：Passage

Agritourism

Agritourism, as it is defined most broadly, involves any agriculturally based activity that brings visitors to a farm or ranch. Agritourism has different definitions in different parts of the world, and sometimes refers specifically to farm stays, as in Italy. Elsewhere, agritourism includes a wide variety of activities, like buying produce directly from a farm stand, navigating a corn maze, picking fruit, feeding animals, or staying at a B&B on a farm.

Agritourism is a form of niche tourism that is considered a growth industry in many parts of the world, including Australia, Canada, the United States, etc. Take the United States. Agritourism is widespread in the United States. Agritourists can choose from a wide range of activities that include picking fruits and vegetables, riding horses, tasting honey, learning about wine and cheesemaking, or shopping in farm gift shops and farm stands for local and regional produce or hand-crafted gifts.

According to the USDA Cooperative State Research, Education and Extension Service, " Tourism is becoming increasingly important to the U. S. economy. A conservative estimate from the Federal Reserve Board in Kansas, based on 2000 data, shows that travel and tourism industries accounted for 3.6 percent of all U. S. employment. Even more telling, data from the Travel Industry Association of America indicate that 1 out of every 18 people in the U. S. has a job directly resulting from travel expenditures."

According to the Small Farm Center at the University of California, "Agricultural tourism, or agritourism, is one alternative for improving the incomes and potential economic viability of small farms and rural communities. Some forms of agritourism enterprises are well developed in California, including fairs and festivals." The UC Small Farm Center has developed a California Agritourism Database that "provides visitors and potential entrepreneurs with information about existing agritourism locations throughout the state".

People have become more interested in how their food is produced. They want to meet farmers and processors and talk with them about what goes into food production. For many people who visit farms, especially children, the visit marks the first time they see the source of their food, be it a dairy cow, an ear of corn growing in a field, or an apple they can pick right off a tree. So for children and adults like, agritourism proves to be a trip of relaxation and rest, and of education as well.

第9单元
银行业务

At the Bank

课文 1　Text A

Section I: Dialog

Interpret the following dialog alternatively into English and Chinese.

顾客：Hello, sir. I'd like to open an account with your bank.

银行职员：好的，小姐。我行有定活两便、通知存款和活期存款3种。您选哪一种？

顾客：Current deposit is fine.

银行职员：小姐，先填一下存款单。

顾客：Where can I get it, sir?

银行职员：在那边的柜台上。

顾客：OK. Got it. Just a moment. All right. Here you are.

银行职员：我们还需要您的护照。

顾客：Oh, where is it? I know I have it. It must be somewhere in my purse. Yes, here it is.

银行职员：谢谢，小姐。

顾客：Is there a minimum for the first deposit?

银行职员：是的，最低1元。

顾客：I see.

银行职员：为了确保存款的安全，您需要设置一个密码，一个6位数的密码。小姐，开始设置吧。

顾客：OK. Done.

银行职员：现在重新键入密码，小姐。

顾客：Again?

银行职员：是的，确认一下。

顾客：OK. Done.

银行职员：好的。您现在想存多少钱？

顾客：2,000 yuan.

银行职员：好的。请在这份文件上签字，小姐。

顾客：Where?

银行职员：在虚线上，小姐。

顾客：I see. OK. Here you are.

银行职员：谢谢。行了。小姐，这是您的存折和护照。

顾客：Thank you. So I can transfer my money in this account into a US account?

银行职员：是的，小姐。非常简单。
顾客：Thank you.
银行职员：谢谢您。谢谢您选择了我们银行。祝您好运。
顾客：Bye.

Section Ⅱ: Passage
Interpret the following passage into Chinese.

The Great Barrier Reef

The Great Barrier Reef is the world's largest coral reef system composed of over 2,900 individual reefs and 900 islands stretching for over 2,300 kilometers. The reef is located in the Coral Sea, off the coast of Queensland, Australia.

The Great Barrier Reef is the world's biggest single structure made by living organisms. This reef structure is built by billions of tiny organisms. It supports a wide diversity of life and was selected as a World Heritage Site in 1981.

The Great Barrier Reef has long been known to and used by the Aboriginal Australian and Torres Strait Islander peoples, and is an important part of local groups' cultures and spirituality. The reef is a very popular destination for tourists.

The land that formed the substrate of the current Great Barrier Reef was a coastal plain formed from the eroded sediments of the Great Dividing Range. According to the Great Barrier Reef Marine Park Authority, the current living reef structure is believed to have begun growing on the older platform about 20,000 years ago.

From 20,000 years ago until 6,000 years ago, sea level rose steadily. As it rose, the corals could then grow higher on the hills of the coastal plain. By around 13,000 years ago the sea level was only 60 meters lower than the present day, and corals began to grow around the hills of the coastal plain, which were, by then, continental islands. As the sea level rose further still, most of the continental islands were submerged. The corals could then overgrow the hills, to form the present cays and reefs.

The Great Barrier Reef supports a diversity of life, including many vulnerable or endangered species, some of which may be endemic to the reef system. It boasts 30 species of whales, dolphins, and porpoises, large populations of dugongs, more than 1,500 fish species, 17 species of sea snakes, 6 species of sea turtles, 7 species of frog, 215 species of birds, 15 species of seagrass in beds that attract the dugongs and turtles, and provide fish habitat, around 125 species of shark, stingray, skates or chimaera, close to 5,000 species of mollusc, 49 species of pipefish, 9 species of seahorse, 330 species of ascidians, and some saltwater crocodiles. It also supports 2,195 known plant species, including 500 species of marine algae or seaweed.

All in all, the Great Barrier Reef, labeled as one of the seven natural wonders of the world by CNN, is larger than the Great Wall of China and the only living thing on earth visible from space.

Section Ⅲ: Passage
Interpret the following passage into English.

野生动物旅游

野生动物旅游可以是一个生态和动物友好型旅游，因为动物通常出现在自然栖息地上。简单来说，野生动物旅游就是在野生动物的自然栖息地上观看动物。野生动物旅游在许多国家都是旅游业的一个重要组成部分，包括许多非洲国家、南美国家、澳大利亚、印度、加拿大、印度尼西亚、孟加拉国、马来西亚、马尔代夫等。近几年来，它在全球各地都经历了戏剧性的迅速增长，与生态旅游和可持续旅游密切相关。

野生动物旅游也是一个价值数百万美元的行业，提供定制化旅游套餐和狩猎之旅。

和任何东西一样，野生动物旅游有积极的方面，也有消极的方面。

积极的方面主要如下。第一，许多生态旅馆的业主或野生动物景点都极力保护和恢复动物的天然栖息地。第二，许多野生动物公园和动物园都把繁殖稀有物种和濒危物种当作主要的活动，并尽可能把它们的后代送到合适的栖息地上。第三，一些野生动物游客为保护工作捐出善款。第四，一本好的野生动物指南能让人更好地了解当地的野生动物及其生态需求，让游客在充分认识的基础上纠正自己的行为，决定支持何种政治举措。第五，一些野生动物旅游业务有助于监测野生动物的数量，促进一般性的野生动物保护研究。第六，经常把游客带到某些地区可能会使大型动物偷猎者或为了黑市交易偷猎小型动物的人难以下手。

另一方面，野生动物旅游也有一些负面影响。野生动物旅游会给自然栖息地上的动物带来极大的干扰。越来越多的人喜欢到发展中国家去旅游，导致这些地区大兴土木，建造度假村和酒店，这种现象在热带雨林和红树林地区尤为明显。观赏野生动物会把动物吓跑，干扰其捕食和繁殖，迫使其适应人类的打扰。例如，在肯尼亚，野生动物观察员的出现会把猎豹从它们的保护地上赶跑，增加近亲繁殖的风险，进一步危及该物种的生存。

野生动物旅游对野生动物的影响取决于旅游发展的规模以及野生动物对人类的反应和适应能力。当旅游活动发生在动物生命周期的敏感时期（如产卵季节），当为了识别动物或摄影而近距离接触野生动物时，干扰的可能性就变得很大。不过，并非所有动物都怕游客，甚至在游人如织的地方也是如此。

游客寻找野生动物进行拍摄或狩猎活动会影响动物的狩猎方式、进食方式及其生殖繁衍。有些活动甚至可能对行为关系和生态关系造成长期影响。

游客人工喂养野生动物可能对其社会行为模式产生严重后果。动物会离开自己的领地，到那些可以从游客手中求来食物的地方，这对一些野生动物的成功繁殖造成负面影响。人工喂养也可能导致动物完全丧失正常的进食行为。

野生动物旅游也会造成动物之间特定关系的中断。例如，当游客出现时，格陵兰雌海豹对幼崽的照顾明显不够，那些依旧和幼崽待在一起的雌海豹照顾幼崽的时间也大幅度减少，它们会花更多的时间去观看游客。还有一个风险，就是它们会不认幼崽，使之更容易受到捕食者的攻击。同样令人担忧的是观赏鲸鱼。鲸鱼幼崽通常与母亲保持不断的身体接触，然而，一旦分开，它们就会依附在船身上。

最后，野生动物游客对某些物种的观赏会使得该物种更容易受到捕食者的攻击。目前，这一现象在鸟类、爬行动物和哺乳动物方面均有记载。

Section Ⅰ：Dialog

顾客：先生，您好。我想开个账户。

银行职员：OK, miss. We have variable term deposit, notice deposit and current deposit here. Which one would you like?

顾客：活期就成。

银行职员：Fill out a deposit slip first, miss.

顾客：哪儿有？

银行职员：On the counter over there.

顾客：好的，找到了。稍等。好了，给您。

银行职员：You also need to show us your passport, miss.

顾客：噢，哪儿去了？ 我知道我带了。肯定在我包里。嗯，在这儿呢。

银行职员：Thank you, miss.

顾客：第一次存款有什么最低限额吗？

银行职员：Yes, the minimum amount is 1 yuan.

顾客：知道了。

银行职员：To ensure the safety of your money, you are supposed to set a PIN number, a 6-digit one. Go ahead, miss.

顾客：好的。好了。

银行职员：Now key in the PIN number again, miss.

顾客：重新输入？

银行职员：Yes. Just to confirm the password.

顾客：好的。好了。

银行职员：Good. Now how much money would you like to deposit into the account, miss?

顾客：2000元。

银行职员：OK. Please sign this document, miss.

顾客：在哪儿？

银行职员：On the dotted line, miss.

顾客：知道了。好了。给您。

银行职员：Thank you. That's it. Here's your passbook and passport, miss.

顾客：谢谢。现在我可以把这个账户上的钱打入我美国的账户了吗？

银行职员：Yes, miss. And it's very easy.

顾客：谢谢。

银行职员：Thank you. Thanks for choosing our bank. Good luck.

顾客：再见。

Section Ⅱ：Passage

大 堡 礁

大堡礁是世界上最大的珊瑚礁系统，由2900多个珊瑚礁和900个岛屿组成，绵延2300千米。大堡礁位于澳大利亚昆士兰沿岸的珊瑚海。

大堡礁是世界上生物体构成的最大的单一结构。这种珊瑚结构是由数十亿微小生物构成的。这里生活着各种各样的生物，1981年入选世界文化遗产名录。

大堡礁长期以来就为澳大利亚土著居民和托雷斯海峡岛民所知晓并加以利用，是当地部落文化和精神信仰的重要组成部分，是颇受欢迎的旅游景点。

今日大堡礁的基底是由滨海平原构成的，而该滨海平原又是由大分水岭被侵蚀的沉积物构成的。根据大堡礁海洋公园管理局的说法，当前的活体礁结构据信约在20000年前就已经开始在更古老的礁石上生长了。

从20000年前到6000年前，海平面不断上升。海平面上升了，珊瑚可以在滨海平原上地势更高的地方生长。约13000年前，海平面只比今天低60米，珊瑚开始在滨海平原地势较高的地方周围生长。那时的滨海平原是陆边岛。随着海平面的进一步上升，大多数陆边岛都被海水淹没。珊瑚继续生长，超过地势较高的地方，形成今天的珊瑚礁。

大堡礁周边生活着各种各样的生物，包括许多脆弱的或濒危物种，其中一些可能是大堡礁特有的物种。这里有30种鲸鱼、海豚、鼠海豚、数量巨大的儒艮、1500多种鱼、17种海蛇、6种海龟、7种青蛙、215种鸟，礁床上有15种吸引儒艮和海龟的海草。这里是鱼类的栖息地，约有125种鲨鱼、黄貂鱼、鳐鱼或银鲛、近5000种软体动物、49种尖嘴鱼、9种海马、330种海鞘和一些海洋鳄鱼。此外，还有2195种已知植物物种，其中包括500种海洋藻类或海草。

总之，被美国有线新闻网评为世界七大自然奇观之一的大堡礁比中国的长城规模还要大，是从太空上可以见到的地球上唯一的生物。

Section Ⅲ：Passage

Wildlife Tourism

Wildlife tourism can be an eco and animal friendly tourism, usually showing animals in their natural habitat. Wildlife tourism, in its simplest sense, is watching wild animals in their natural habitat. Wildlife tourism is an important part of the tourism industries in many countries including many African and South American countries, Australia, India, Canada, Indonesia, Bangladesh, Malaysia and Maldives among many. It has experienced a dramatic and rapid growth in recent years worldwide and is closely aligned to eco-tourism and sustainable-tourism.

Wildlife tourism is also a multi-million dollar industry offering customized tour packages and safaris.

Like anything, wildlife tourism has its positive and negative impacts.

The positive impacts are mainly as follows. First, many owners of eco-accommodation or wildlife attractions preserve and restore native habitats on their properties. Second, many wildlife parks and zoos breed rare and endangered species as a major part of their activities, and release the progeny when possible into suitable habitat. Third, some wildlife tourists contribute monetary donations to conservation efforts. Fourth, a good wildlife guide will impart a deeper understanding of the local wildlife and its ecological needs, which may give visitors a more informed base on which to subsequently modify their behavior and decide what political moves to support. Fifth, some wildlife tourism operations contribute to monitoring of wildlife numbers or general research relevant to conservation. Sixth, bringing tourists regularly into some areas may make it more difficult for poachers of large animals or those who collect smaller species for the black market.

On the other hand, wildlife tourism also has some negative impacts. Wildlife tourism can cause significant disturbances to animals in their natural habitats. The growing interest in traveling to developing countries has created a boom in resort and hotel construction, particularly on rain forest and mangrove forest lands. Wildlife viewing can scare away animals, disrupt their feeding and nesting sites, or acclimate them to the presence of people. In Kenya, for example, wildlife-observer disruption drives cheetahs off their reserves, increasing the risk of inbreeding and further endangering the species.

The effect that wildlife tourism will have on wildlife depends on the scale of tourist development and the behavior and resilience of wildlife to the presence of humans. When tourist activities occur during sensitive times of the life cycle, for example, during nesting season, and when they involve close approaches to wildlife for the purpose of identification or photography, the potential for disturbance is high. Not all species appear to be disturbed by tourists even within heavily visited areas.

The pressures of tourists searching out wildlife to photograph or hunt can adversely affect hunting and feeding patterns, and the breeding success of some species. Some may even have long-term implications for behavioral and ecological relationships.

Artificial feeding of wildlife by tourists can have severe consequences for social behavior patterns. Territories were abandoned in favor of sites where food could be begged from tourists, and this has had a negative effect on the breeding success of some wild animals. Artificial feeding can also result in a complete loss of normal feeding behaviors.

Wildlife tourism also causes disruption to intra-specific relationships. For instance, attendance by female harp seals to their pups declined when tourists were present and those females remaining with their pups spent significantly less time nursing and more time watching the tourists. There is also a risk of the young not being recognized, and being more exposed to predator attacks. A similar concern has been expressed over whale watching. Whale calves normally maintain constant body contact with their mothers, but, when separated, can transfer their attachment to the side of the boat.

Finally, the viewing of certain species by wildlife tourists makes the species more vulnerable to predators. Evidence of this phenomenon has been recorded in birds, reptiles and mammals.

课文 2　Text B

Section Ⅰ: Dialog
Interpret the following dialog alternatively into English and Chinese.

顾客: Hello, miss. Can I change some money here?
银行职员: 当然。您想兑换哪种货币?
顾客: Renminbi.
银行职员: 您想兑换多少?
顾客: Could you please tell me today's exchange rate between Renminbi and the US dollar?
银行职员: 请稍等。100 美元兑换 689.27 元。
顾客: Then change these 820 dollars to Renminbi, please.
银行职员: 好的。一共 5652 元。您想要什么面值的?
顾客: Well, twenty-five 100s, fifty 50s, and some smaller bills, please.
银行职员: 好的,先生,请稍等。看,25 张 100 元的,50 张 50 元的,这些是您要的小面额的,包括 20 元和 10 元的。剩下的都是 1 元的。
顾客: Thank you.
银行职员: 先生,还需要其他服务吗?
顾客: Yes, I also have some Japanese yen here, as I just came from Japan. Would you please change the Japanese yen into Renminbi?
银行职员: 可以。先生,您想兑换多少日元?
顾客: 8,000.
银行职员: 好的。一共是 488 元。您想要什么面值的?
顾客: I prefer smaller bills.
银行职员: 10 元的和 1 元的怎么样?
顾客: That will be fine.
银行职员: 好的。这是 40 张 10 元的,剩下的都是 1 元的。
顾客: Thank you very much.
银行职员: 不谢。

Section Ⅱ: Passage
Interpret the following passage into Chinese.

Venice

Venice is a city in northeastern Italy sited on a group of 118 small islands separated by canals and linked by bridges. It is located in the Venetian Lagoon which stretches along the shoreline, between the mouths of the Po and the Piave Rivers. Venice is renowned for the beauty of its setting, its architecture and its artworks. The city in its entirety is listed as a World Heritage Site, along with its lagoon.

Venice is one of the most important tourist destinations in the world for its celebrated art and architecture. The city has an average of 50,000 tourists a day, according to a 2007 estimate. In 2006, it was the world's 28th most internationally visited city, with 2.927 million international arrivals that year. It is regarded as one of the world's most beautiful cities.

The name is derived from the ancient Veneti people who inhabited the region by the 10th century B.C. The city historically was the capital of the Republic of Venice. Venice has been known as the "Queen of the Adriatic", "City of Water", "City of Masks", "City of Bridges", "The Floating City", and "City of Canals". It has also been described by *The New York Times* as "undoubtedly the most beautiful city built by man", and "one of Europe's most romantic cities".

The Republic of Venice was a major maritime power during the Middle Ages and Renaissance, and a staging area for the Crusades as well as a very important center of commerce and art in the 13th century up to the end of the 17th century. This made Venice a wealthy city throughout most of its history. It is also known for its several important artistic movements, especially the Renaissance period. Venice has played an important role in the history of symphonic and operatic music, and it is the birthplace of Antonio Vivaldi.

Tourism has been a major sector of Venetian industry since the 18th century, when it was a major center for the Grand Tour, with its beautiful cityscape, uniqueness, and rich musical and artistic cultural heritage. In the 19th century, it became a fashionable centre for the rich and famous, often staying or dining at luxury establishments. It continued being a fashionable city in vogue right into the early 20th century. In the 1980s, the Carnival of Venice was revived and the city has become a major center of international conferences and festivals, such as the prestigious Venice Biennale and the Venice Film Festival, which attract visitors from all over the world for their theatrical, cultural, cinematic, artistic, and musical productions.

Today, there are numerous attractions in Venice, such as St Mark's Basilica, the Grand Canal, and the Piazza San Marco. The Lido di Venezia is also a popular international luxury destination, attracting thousands of actors, critics, and celebrities mainly from the cinematic industry. The city also relies heavily on the cruise business.

Section Ⅲ: Passage
Interpret the following passage into English.

生 态 旅 游

生态旅游是一种旅游形式，包括参观脆弱、原始和人迹罕至的自然区，是为常规的商业旅游提供的一种选择。这是一种小范围的环保旅游，目的也许是为了教育旅客，为生态保护提供资金，直接造福当地社区的经济发展和政治权利，或培养人们尊重人权、尊重不同文化的意识。自20世纪80年代以来，生态旅游已经被环保人士视为一个至关重要的举措，这样，我们的后代就可以享受相对原生态的旅游目的地了。

一般来说，生态旅游关心的是自然环境中有生命的东西。生态旅游重点关注社会责任型旅行、个人成长和环境的可持续性等问题。生态旅游的目的地通常是以动植物和文化遗产为主要景点的地方。生态旅游的目的，是让游客认识到人类对环境的影响，促使人们更加珍惜人类的自然栖息地。

社会责任型生态旅游项目包括那些尽量消除传统旅游对环境的负面影响、尽量保持当地人民文化完整性的项目。所以，除了考虑环境因素和文化因素以外，生态旅游的一个重要组成部分就是倡导回收利用、节能节水，为当地社区创造经济机会。正因如此，生态旅游常常得到环保与社会责任倡导者的共鸣。

"生态旅游"这一术语，一如"可持续旅游"一样，在许多人眼里是个矛盾说法。一般而言，旅游依靠的是航空运输，但同时旅游反过来又会增加航空运输的班次，因而会大大增加温室气体的排放，进入平流层（同温层）之后，马上产生聚热现象，导致全球变暖和气候变化。此外，"可持续旅游的总体效果是消极的。正如生态旅游一样，慈善的面具下掩藏着赤裸裸的眼前私利"。

Section Ⅰ: Dialog

顾客：小姐，您好。我可以在此兑换一些货币吗？

银行职员：Sure. What kind of currency do you want?

顾客：人民币。

银行职员：How much do you want to change?

顾客：请告诉我今天人民币和美元的汇率是多少。

银行职员：Hold on a second. It's 689.27 yuan for 100 dollars.

顾客：那么，请把这820美元兑换成人民币。

银行职员：OK. That's 5652 yuan. In what denominations do you prefer?

顾客：嗯，25张100元的，50张50元的，其余的都要小额面值的。

银行职员：OK, sir. Just a minute. Look, here are 25 100s, 50 50s, and these are the smaller bills you want, including 20s and 10s. The rest are 1-yuan bills.

顾客：谢谢。

银行职员：Anything else, sir?

顾客：是的。我还有一些日元，因为我刚从日本过来。请把这些日元兑换成人民币。

银行职员：Sure. How much yen do you want to change, sir?

顾客：8000。

银行职员：OK. That's 488 yuan. How would you like them?

顾客：我喜欢小额面值的。

银行职员：How about 10-yuan bills and 1-yuan bills?

顾客：很好。

银行职员：OK. Here are 40 10-yuan bills, and the rest are 1-yuan bills.

顾客：多谢。

银行职员：You are very welcome.

Section Ⅱ: Passage

威 尼 斯

威尼斯是意大利东北部城市，坐落在118个小岛上。小岛被运河隔开，但又通过桥梁连接在一起。威尼斯位于沿着海岸延伸的威尼斯泻湖上，介于波河和皮亚韦河的河口之间。威尼斯以其美丽的环境、宏伟的建筑和精美的艺术品而名闻天下。整个城市及其泻湖入选世界文化遗产名录。

威尼斯以其著名的艺术和建筑成为世界上最重要的旅游目的地之一。根据2007年的估计,威尼斯平均每天接待游客5万多人。2006年,它成为全球第28个国际游客最多的城市,当年的外国游客人数达到292.7万。威尼斯被认为是世界上最美丽的城市之一。

威尼斯这个名字来源于公元前10世纪居住在此地的古代威尼西亚人,这个城市历史上是威尼斯共和国的首都。威尼斯素有"亚得里亚海皇后""水之城""面具之城""桥之城""漂浮的城市"和"运河之城"之称。《纽约时报》形容它为"当之无愧的最美丽的人造城市"和"欧洲最浪漫的城市之一"。

威尼斯共和国是中世纪和文艺复兴时期一个重要的海上强国,是十字军东征时的集结地,也是13世纪到17世纪末一个非常重要的商业中心和艺术中心,这使得威尼斯在历史上大多数时期都是一个非常富裕的城市。威尼斯也因几次重要的艺术运动(特别是文艺复兴)而闻名。威尼斯在交响乐和歌剧音乐的历史上发挥了重要作用,也是安东尼奥·维瓦尔第的诞生地。

18世纪以来,旅游一直是威尼斯的主要行业。当时,其美丽的市容、与众不同的特性以及丰富多彩的音乐艺术文化遗产使其成为"大旅游"的重要中心。19世纪,它变成了富人和名人惠顾的时尚中心,他们经常在豪华场所下榻或进餐。直到20世纪初,它一直是一个时尚之都。20世纪80年代,威尼斯狂欢节重获新生,整个城市马上成为一个重要的国际会议中心和节日中心,如著名的威尼斯双年展和威尼斯电影节以其戏剧、文化、电影、艺术和音乐作品吸引着来自世界各地的游客。

今天,威尼斯有很多景点,如圣马克大教堂、大运河、圣马可广场等。威尼斯利多岛也是一个备受欢迎的国际豪华旅游胜地,吸引了数以千计的演员、评论家等电影界的名人。威尼斯也在很大程度上依赖于水上航游。

Section Ⅲ: Passage

Ecotourism

Ecotourism is a form of tourism involving visiting fragile, pristine, and relatively undisturbed natural areas, intended as a low-impact and often small scale alternative to standard commercial tourism. Its purpose may be to educate the traveler, to provide funds for ecological conservation, to directly benefit the economic development and political empowerment of local communities, or to foster respect for different cultures and for human rights. Since the 1980s ecotourism has been considered a critical endeavor by environmentalists, so that future generations may experience destinations relatively untouched by human intervention.

Generally, ecotourism deals with living parts of the natural environments. Ecotourism focuses on socially responsible travel, personal growth, and environmental sustainability. Ecotourism typically involves travel to destinations where flora, fauna, and cultural heritage are the primary attractions. Ecotourism is intended to offer tourists insight into the impact of human beings on the environment, and to foster a greater appreciation of our natural habitats.

Responsible ecotourism programs include those that minimize the negative aspects of conventional tourism on the environment and enhance the cultural integrity of local people. Therefore, in addition to evaluating environmental and cultural factors, an integral part of ecotourism is the promotion of recycling, energy efficiency, water conservation, and creation of economic opportunities for local communities. For these reasons, ecotourism often appeals to advocates of environmental and social responsibility.

The term "ecotourism", like "sustainable tourism", is considered by many to be an oxymoron. Tourism in general depends upon and increases air transportation, contributing significantly to greenhouse gas emissions from combustion placed high into the stratosphere where they immediately contribute to the heat trapping phenomenon behind global warming and climate change. Additionally, "the overall effect of sustainable tourism is negative, where, like ecotourism, philanthropic aspirations mask naked immediate self-interest".

第10单元
深度旅游

In-depth Travel

课文 1　Text A

Section Ⅰ: Dialog
Interpret the following dialog alternatively into English and Chinese.

导游：早上好。欢迎来到江苏。我叫凯特，是你们今天的导游。欢迎大家参加我们的周庄一日游。和以往不同的是，今天的旅游叫深度游。

游客：An in-depth tour?

导游：和以往那些走马观花式的观光游不同，深度游就是一次外出只选择一个地方，而不是在一个相对有限的时段内跑数个景点的旅游。比如，今天我们只有一站，那就是周庄。

游客：That is to say, we have plenty of time to learn about the history, culture, habits and insititutions of a place.

导游：没错。请问，您是第一次来江苏吗？

游客：Yes. We all are here for the first time. I only heard that Zhouzhuang is a very special place, and that's all I know about it.

导游：周庄是一座江南小镇，有"中国第一水乡"的美誉，是国家 5A 级景区。

游客：It must have a long history.

导游：是啊。周庄始建于 1086 年，距今有 900 多年的历史。准确地说，是 930 年了。

游客：That's some history.

导游：周庄位于昆山境内，苏州东南 38 千米处。

游客：Is it different from any other water town?

导游：它是江南六大古镇之一，于 2003 年被评为中国历史文化名镇。周庄有着深厚的文化底蕴、独特的人文景观、保存完好的古代民居以及优美的水上风光，素有"东方威尼斯"之称。

游客：The Venice of the East? It seems that we have come to the right place. I love water towns.

导游：周庄 60% 以上的民居仍为明清风格的建筑，仅 0.47 平方千米的古镇有近百座古典宅院和 60 多个砖雕门楼。

游客：To leave such a place intact in todaty's rapid advance of urbanization? That's incredible!

导游：周庄还保存了 14 座各具特色的古桥，有很多景点，如沈厅、富安桥、双桥等。

游客：Amazing! Are there any recreational programs, please?

导游：有很多。白天可以欣赏鱼鹰表演，晚上可以乘船夜游，听昆曲。

游客：Kunqu? What's that?

导游：昆曲是中国最古老的剧种，可以追溯到唐宋时期，为"百戏之祖"，是"人类口述与非物质文化遗产代表作"。

游客：China is well known for its delicious food. Zhouzhuang must boast lots of it.

导游：当然。最著名的是万三蹄和三味圆。前者因元明时江南首富沈万三得名，后者是当地人的家庭美食。

游客：Thanks for your introduction, Kate. You must be tired. You will give us a detailed introduction when we get there. So take a break and save your voice.

导游：那我就恭敬不如从命了。

Section Ⅱ：Passage

Interpret the following passage into Chinese.

World Heritage Sites

A UNESCO World Heritage Site is a place (such as a forest, mountain, lake, island, desert, monument, building, complex, or city) that is listed by United Nations Educational, Scientific and Cultural Organization (UNESCO) as of special cultural or worldwide significance. The list is maintained by the international World Heritage Programme, administered by the UNESCO World Heritage Committee, composed of 21 State Parties, which are elected by their General Assembly.

The programme catalogues, names, and conserves sites of outstanding cultural or natural importance to the common heritage of humanity. Under certain conditions, listed sites can obtain funds from the World Heritage Fund. The programme was founded with the International Convention Concerning the Protection of the World Cultural and Natural Heritage, which was adopted by the General Conference of UNESCO in Paris on 16 November 1972. Since then, 190 States Parties have ratified the Convention, making it one of the most adhered to international instruments. Only the Bahamas, Liechtenstein, Nauru, Somalia, South Sudan, Timor-Leste and Tuvalu are not Party to the Convention.

As of 2016, 1052 sites are listed: 814 cultural, 203 natural, and 35 mixed properties, in 165 States Parties. By sites ranked by country, Italy is home to the greatest number of World Heritage Sites with 51 sites, followed by China(50), Spain(45), France(42) and Germany(41).

While each World Heritage Site remains part of the legal territory of the state wherein the site is located, UNESCO considers it in the interest of the international community to preserve each site.

Since joining the International Convention Concerning the Protection of World Cultural and Natural Heritage in 1985, China has 50 world heritage sites to date; of these 35 are cultural heritage sites, 11 are natural heritage sites, and 4 are cultural and natural (mixed) sites, ranking second in the world. Since 2004, China has made the first large-scale renovations on 7 world cultural heritage sites in Beijing — the Ming Tombs, the Great Wall, the Forbidden City, the Temple of Heaven, the Summer Palace, the Grand Canal, and the "Peking Man" site at Zhoukoudian. In addition, China has a rich non-material cultural heritage, with several of them inscribed on UNESCO's list of Masterpieces of the Oral and Intangible Heritage of Humanity.

Section Ⅲ: Passage
Interpret the following passage into English.

养 生 旅 游

养生旅游是通过体育活动、心理活动或精神活动来提高健康水平和幸福感的旅行。养生旅游常常与医疗旅游联系在一起，因为对健康的追求促使人们外出旅游。养生游客往往主动出击，寻求改善或维持健康水平和生活质量，通常专注于预防。相反，医疗游客则一般来说是因为诊断出某种疾病而被动地接受治疗。

在价值3.2万亿美元的全球旅游经济市场中，养生旅游估计达到4386亿美元，占2012年国内、国际旅游支出总额的14%。在亚洲、中东和发展中国家经济增长的背景下，未来5年里，养生旅游有望比整个旅游行业发展快50%。

养生游客通常是高收入者，平均支出超过普通游客130%。国际养生游客每趟平均支出超过普通国际游客65%左右。国内养生游客平均支出超过普通游客150%左右。国内养生旅游市场明显大于国际养生旅游市场，占养生旅游市场的84%，占总支出的68%（总额达到2990亿美元）。国际养生旅游占养生旅游市场的16%，占总支出的32%（总额达到1390亿美元）。

养生旅游市场包括一类游客和二类游客。一类游客旅行的目的就是为了养生，二类游客参加与养生有关的活动，把它当成旅行的一部分。二类游客构成养生旅游和相关支出的主体。前者占87%，后者占86%。

养生游客追求多元化服务，包括健身、运动、美容、健康饮食和体重控制、放松、减压、冥想、瑜伽及健康教育等。养生游客可能会利用传统医学、替代医学、补充医学、草药医学或顺势医学求方治疗。

近 1700 万（40%）美国酒店客人寻求旅行时保持健康的生活方式。全球酒店集团已经开发和推广了许多项目，吸引这些重视健康的客人。这些项目包括健康菜单、放松运动、水疗服务、健身设施、开办健身班等。截至 2012 年，美国 80% 以上的酒店和 90% 以上的高档酒店都提供健身设施。国际上，45% 的酒店客人表示，酒店水疗中心的存在是他们考虑订房的一个重要因素。

健康度假村和休养地提供短期小憩项目以解决特定的健康问题，减轻压力，支持生活方式的改善。

养生旅游倡导者认为，度假能增进身体健康，增加幸福指数，提高办事效率，并且养生旅游能给游客带来一个全新的视角，对其创造力、适应力、解决问题的能力和应对压力的能力都产生积极影响。

Section I: Dialog

导游：Good morning. Welcome to Jiangsu Province. My name is Kate. I'm your tour guide today. Welcome to our one-day visit to Zhouzhuang. But unlike before, today's visit is called an in-depth tour.

游客：深度游？

导游：Unlike the cursory sight-seeing trips before, an in-depth tour is one in which you visit only one place at a time instead of going to different tourist attractions in a limited period of time. Just like today, we have only one stop. That's Zhouzhuang.

游客：也就是说，我们有充足的时间来了解一个地方的历史文化、风土人情了。

导游：Exactly. Well, is this your first trip to Jiangsu Province?

游客：是的，我们都是第一次来。只听说周庄是个很特别的地方，别的就不知道了。

导游：Zhouzhuang is a small town in South China. It is known as the first water town in China. It is classified as a 5A scenic area by the China National Tourism Administration.

游客：那一定有不短的历史了吧？

导游：You are right. Zhouzhuang was built in 1086, and it has a history of more than 900 years. 930, to be exact.

游客：真有年头了。

导游：Zhouzhuang is located within the city of Kunshan, a county-level city, 38 kilometers southeast of the city of Suzhou.

游客：它和别的水乡有什么不同吗？

导游：It is one of the 6 ancient towns in South China, and it was named a Historic and Cultural Town in China in 2003. It is noted for its profound cultural background, unique man-made landscapes, well preserved ancient residential houses and elegant watery views. It has been called the "Venice of the East".

游客：东方威尼斯？看来，我们是来对地方了。我喜欢水乡。

导游：Over 60% of the residential houses are of the architectural styles of the Ming and the Qing Dyansties. And the small ancient town, built on a 0.47-km^2 of land, boasts nearly 100 ancient courtyards and more than 60 gate towers with brick carvings.

游客：在城镇化快速推进的今天，还能有这样的地方，真是不可思议。

导游：Zhouzhuang has kept 14 distinctive ancient bridges. It has many attractions like the Shen House, the Fu'an Bridge, the Twin Bridges, to name but a few.

游客：不得了。请问，有什么娱乐项目吗？

导游：There are lots of them. You can enjoy fish hawks catching fish during the day, and in the evening you can go down the river in a boat and watch the Kunqu opera.

游客：昆曲是什么？

导游：Kunqu is actually the oldest form of opera in China. It goes back to the Tang and Song dynasties and is known as the father of Chinese operas. It is listed by UNESCO as a masterpiece of the Oral and Intangible Heritage of Humanity.

游客：中国人素以美食闻名天下。周庄也有不少吧？

导游：Certainly. The most well-known local dishes are *Wansan Pork Hock* and *Sanwei Gutinous Rice Balls*. The former is named after Wansan Shen, the richest man in the late Yuan and early Ming dynasties in South China, and the latter is an evreyday dish for the locals.

游客：凯特，谢谢你热情洋溢的介绍。累了吧？待会儿到了周庄你还要详细介绍呢。先休息一下，省省嗓子吧。

导游：OK, if you insist.

Section II: Passage

世界遗产名录

联合国教科文组织世界文化遗产是一个地方，如森林、山脉、湖泊、岛屿、沙漠、历史遗迹、建筑、建筑群或城市等。这个地方被联合国教科文组织收录，具有特殊的文化意义或世界意义。该名录由联合国教科文组织世界遗产委员会监管的国际"世界遗产项目"确认，该委员会由 21 个缔约国组成，是由联合国大会选举产生的。

该项目收录、提名、保护在文化方面或自然方面对人类的共同遗产具有重要意义的遗址。在某些情况下，入选的遗址可以获得世界遗产基金。该项目是在《保护世界文化和自然遗产国际公约》通过后启动的，该公约是在联合国教科文组织1972 年 11 月 16 日在巴黎举办的大会上通过的。从那时起，190 个缔约国签署了该公约，使之成为遵守最好的国际契约之一。只有巴哈马群岛、列支敦士登、瑙鲁、索马里、南苏丹、东帝汶和图瓦卢不是该公约的缔约国。

截至 2016 年，共有 1052 处遗址入选。其中，文化遗产 814 处，自然遗产 203 处，双重遗产 35 处，这些遗产分布在 165 个缔约国。按照世界遗产多少排列，意大利位居第一，拥有 51 处，紧随其后是中国（50 处）、西班牙（45 处）、法国（42 处）和德国（41 处）。

虽然每个世界遗产仍然是所在国合法领土的一部分，但是，联合国教科文组织认为，对该遗产的保护符合国际社会的利益。

自从 1985 年加入《保护世界文化和自然遗产国际公约》以来，中国已有 50 处入选世界遗产。其中，文化遗产 35 处，自然遗产 11 处，双重遗产 4 处，排名世界第二。自 2004 年以来，中国首次对北京的 7 处世界文化遗产进行大规模修复，即十三陵、长城、故宫、天坛、颐和园、大运河及周口店"北京人"遗址。此外，中国拥有丰富的非物质文化遗产，其中几项已入选联合国教科文组织"人类口头和非物质遗产代表作名录"。

Section Ⅲ: Passage

Wellness Tourism

Wellness tourism is travel for the purpose of promoting health and well-being through physical, psychological, or spiritual activities. While wellness tourism is often correlated with medical tourism because health interests motivate the traveler, wellness tourists are proactive in seeking to improve or maintain health and quality of life, often focusing on prevention, while medical tourists generally travel reactively to receive treatment for a diagnosed disease or condition.

Within the US $ 3.2 trillion global tourism economy, wellness tourism is estimated to total US $ 438.6 billion or 14 percent of all 2012 domestic and international tourism expenditures. Driven by growth in Asia, the Middle East, and developing countries, wellness tourism is expected to grow 50 percent faster than the overall tourism industry over the next five years.

Wellness tourists are generally high-yield tourists, spending, on average, 130 percent more than the average tourist. International wellness tourists spend approximately 65 percent more per trip than the average international tourist; domestic wellness tourists spend about 150 percent more than the average domestic tourist. Domestic wellness tourism is significantly larger than its international equivalent, representing 84 percent of wellness travel and 68 percent of expenditures (or $299 billion). International wellness tourism represents 16 percent of wellness travel and 32 percent of expenditures ($139 billion market).

The wellness tourism market includes primary and secondary wellness tourists. Primary wellness tourists travel entirely for wellness purposes while secondary wellness tourists engage in wellness-related activities as part of a trip. Secondary wellness tourists constitute the significant majority of total wellness tourism trips (87 percent) and expenditures (86 percent).

Wellness travelers pursue diverse services, including physical fitness and sports; beauty treatments; healthy diet and weight management; relaxation and stress relief; meditation; yoga; and health-related education. Wellness travelers may seek procedures or treatments using conventional, alternative, complementary, herbal, or homeopathic medicine.

Almost 17 million (40 percent) of US hotel guests seek to maintain a healthy lifestyle while traveling. Global hotel groups have developed and promoted programs to attract these health-conscious guests. Programs include healthy menu options, relaxation programs, spa services, and fitness facilities and classes. As of 2012, over 80 percent of US hotels and over 90 percent of upscale US hotels offered fitness facilities. Internationally, 45 percent of hotel guests indicated that the existence of a hotel spa was an important factor in their booking decision.

Wellness resorts and retreats offer short-term, residential programs to address specific health concerns, reduce stress, or support lifestyle improvement.

Wellness tourism advocates suggest that vacations improve physical well-being, happiness, and productivity, citing that health-oriented trips give travelers a fresh perspective and positively affect creativity, resilience, problem solving, and capacity for coping with stress.

课文 2　Text B

Section Ⅰ：Dialog

Interpret the following dialog alternatively into English and Chinese.

导游：大家好。今天我们去八大关。

游客：Badaguan? Does it have any special meaning?

导游：您问对了。"关"在汉语中是"关隘"的意思。那里有 8 条马路，都是以中国古代著名关隘命名的。

游客：So Badaguan means 8 passes?

导游：是的。后来又增加了 2 条马路。但是，景区的名字还是延续以往的叫法。

游客：I see.

导游：八大关是中国著名的疗养区，面积 70 余公顷。新中国成立前，那里是官僚资本家的别墅区。新中国成立后，人民政府对八大关进行了全面修缮，使其成为中国重要的疗养区之一，许多国家领导人及重要的国际友人曾在那里下榻。

游客：So it must be a very quiet and picturesque place.

导游：没错。"八大关"的特点是把公园与庭院融合在一起。到处是郁郁葱葱的树木，四季盛开的鲜花，10 条马路的行道树品种各异。

游客：Sounds fascinating.

导游：韶关路全植碧桃，春季开花，粉红如带；正阳关路遍种紫薇，夏天盛开；居庸关路是五角枫，秋季霜染枫红，平添美色；紫荆关路两侧是成排的雪松，四季常青；宁武关路则是海棠，从春初到秋末花开不断，被誉为"花街"。

游客：Flower road! I love getting the family outdoors and experiencing the beauty of Nature.

导游：在八大关东北角又新植了一片桃林，成为春季人们踏青的又一好去处。西南角则绿柏夹道，成双的绿柏隔成了一个个"包厢"，为许多情侣们所钟爱，因此，那里又被称为"爱情角"。

游客：What a romantic place!

导游：此外，"八大关"的建筑造型独特，汇聚了众多的建筑风格，故有"万国建筑博览会"之称。那里集中了俄罗斯、英国、法国、德国、美国、丹麦、希腊、西班牙、瑞士、日本等 20 多个国家的各式建筑风格。

游客：Over 20 countries. So it is comparable to The Bund in Shanghai.

导游：说得对。八大关风格多样的建筑使那里成为中国电影外景的最佳选择。迄今为止，40 多部电影和 20 多部电视剧都在那里拍摄完成，很多歌星的 MTV 外景也选在那里。

游客：Amazing! I know from the internet that Qingdao enjoys an agreeable climate all year round. I guess that is also a plus for the city and the Badaguan Scenic Area.

导游：是啊。青岛的气候属于温带季风性气候，三面环海，一面靠山。独特的地理格局使青岛又具有了海洋性气候的特点。这里冬无严寒，夏无酷暑。良好的气候使青岛非常适合度假。所以，青岛还有"东方瑞士"的美誉。

游客：Oh, I'm jealous.

导游：相信你一定会流连忘返的。

游客：I think so, too.

Section Ⅱ: Passage
Interpret the following passage into Chinese.

Sustainable Tourism

There has been an up-trend in tourism over the last few decades, especially in Europe, where international travel for short breaks is common. Tourists have a wide range of budgets and tastes, and a wide variety of resorts and hotels have developed to cater for them. For example, some people prefer simple beach vacations, while others want more specialized holidays, quieter resorts, family-oriented holidays or niche market-targeted destination hotels.

The developments in technology and transport infrastructure, such as jumbo jets, low-cost airlines and more accessible airports have made many types of tourism more affordable. The WHO estimated in 2009 that there are around half a million people on board aircraft at any given time. There have also been changes in lifestyle, for example, some retirement-age people sustain year-round tourism. This is facilitated by internet sales of tourist services. Some sites have now started to offer dynamic packaging, in which an inclusive price is quoted for a tailor-made package requested by the customer upon impulse.

On the other hand, with the rapid development of tourism, more and more people are concerned about the negative impacts tourism will have on the ecosystem. Hence the concept of sustainable tourism. "Sustainable tourism" is the concept of visiting a place as a tourist and trying to make only a positive impact on the environment, society and economy. Tourism can involve primary transportation to the general location, local transportation, accommodations, entertainment, recreation and shopping. It can be related to travel for leisure, business and what is called VFR (visiting friends and relatives). There is now broad consensus that tourism development should be sustainable.

Sustainable tourism is envisaged as leading to management of all resources in such a way that economic, social and aesthetic needs can be fulfilled while maintaining cultural integrity, essential ecological processes, biological diversity and life support systems.

Sustainable development implies meeting the needs of the present without compromising the ability of future generations to meet their own needs.

Sustainable tourism can be seen as having regard to ecological and socio-cultural carrying capacities and includes involving the community of the destination in tourism development planning. It also involves integrating tourism to match current economic and growth policies so as to mitigate some of the negative economic and social impacts of "mass tourism". Some people advocate the use of an "ecological approach" to consider both "plants" and "people" when implementing the sustainable tourism development process. This is in contrast to the "boosterism" and "economic" approaches to tourism planning, neither of which consider the detrimental ecological or sociological impacts of tourism development to a destination.

Section Ⅲ: Passage
Interpret the following passage into English.

文化遗产旅游

文化遗产旅游，或者干脆叫作遗产旅游，是旅游的一个分支，它所关注的是旅游地的文化遗产。美国国家历史建筑保护信托会给遗产旅游下的定义是，遗产旅游就是"外出体验真正代表过去人和事的地方、手工艺品和活动，包括文化、历史和自然资源等"。

文化一直是旅游的重要对象，这一点从欧洲16世纪的"大旅游"开始就已经得到证明。到了20世纪，有人开始声称，文化不再是旅游的目的，旅游本身就是文化。文化景点在旅游的各个层面都发挥着重要作用，从全球性的世界文化景点到各地的特色景点，无不如此。

据某些专家的看法，文化、遗产和艺术历来是旅游目的地最吸引人的地方。然而，近年来，"文化"得以重新发掘，成为一种重要的营销手段，来吸引那些对遗产和艺术情有独钟的游客。事实上，文化遗产旅游是旅游业增长最快的部分，因为现在的趋势是游客的分类越来越细。这一趋势非常明显，因为寻求冒险、文化、历史、考古、与当地居民互动的游客越来越多。

文化遗产旅游之所以重要，有很多原因。它对经济和社会带来积极影响，建立和明确身份，有助于保护文化遗产，促进人们之间的和谐与理解，尊重文化，使旅游业不断出新。然而，文化遗产旅游也可能在不同的利益相关者之间造成紧张，甚至冲突。

文化遗产旅游有很多目标必须在可持续发展的背景下才能得以实现，如文化资源的保护、文化资源的准确诠释、真正的游客体验以及文化资源的收入增值。因此，我们可以看到，文化遗产旅游涉及的不仅仅是身份的识别、管理以及传统价值观的保护，它还必须在营销和推广的基础上参与了解旅游对社区和地区的影响，实现经济效益和社会效益，为保护提供财政资源。遗产旅游包括参观历史名胜或工业场所，这可能包括古老的运河、铁路、战场等。总体目标是对历史的了解。它也可以指把一个地方营销给那些根在当地的散居侨民。

参考答案

Section Ⅰ: Dialog

导游: Hello, folks. We are going to Badaguan today.

游客: 八大关？这个名字有什么特殊含义吗？

导游: That's a good question. Guan means "a mountain pass" or "a strategic post" in Chinese. There are 8 roads there, and each was named after a famous pass in ancient China.

游客: 所以，八大关的意思是8个关隘？

导游: You got it. Two more roads were built later. But the name of the scenic area remains the same.

游客: 明白了。

导游: Badaguan or the Eight Passes is a well-known convalescence area in China. It covers an area of over 70 hectares. Before 1949, it was a villa district for bureaucrat capitalists. After the founding of New China, a complete renovation was done by the People's Government and the area was turned into one of the major sanitarial districts in China. Quite a few state leaders and international friends stayed there.

游客: 所以，那一定是个景色优美、幽静宜人的地方。

导游: You are right. The Badaguan Scenic Area integrates the features of parks and courtyards. You can see green trees everywhere. Flowers are in bloom all year round. And the trees lining the 10 roads are of various species.

游客：听起来很迷人。

导游：Shaoguan Road is lined with flowering peach trees, which blossom in Spring, like pink ribbons, and Zhengyangguan Road, with crape myrtles, which bloom in Summer. The trees lining Juyongguan Road are acer monoes, which add beauty to the road with their red leaves in Fall. The trees on both sides of Zijingguan Road are cedars or white pines, which remain green throughout the year. Ningwuguan Road is planted with cherry-apple trees, which flower from early Spring to late Fall. Therefore it is known as the Flower Road.

游客：花街？ 我非常喜欢带家人出来，领略大自然的美景。

导游：A large peach grove was planted in the northeast corner of the Badaguan Scenic Area not long ago, which has become an ideal place for those who enjoy an outing in Spring. In the southwest of the area, you can see green cypresses lining the roads, forming "boxes", which are favored by sweethearts on a date. As a result, that area is called the "Love Corner".

游客：好浪漫的地方！

导游：Besides, the buildings there are uniquely shaped, with a large collection of architectural styles. So it is crowned as an Expo of World Architecture. You can find the architectural styles of over 20 countries incluindg Russia, the UK, France, Germany, the USA, Denmark, Greece, Spain, Switerland, and Japan.

游客：20多个国家！ 因此，它可以和上海的外滩媲美了。

导游：Exactly. The various architectural styles there have made Badaguan the best place for location shooting in China. So far, more than 40 movies and 20-odd teleplays have been shot there. It is also a location shooting place for the music videos of famous singers.

游客：真不得了！ 我在网上看到，青岛一年四季气候宜人。我想，这对青岛和八大关景区来说，也加分不少吧！

导游：You can say that again. Qingdao enjoys a temperate monsoon climate. It is surrounded by sea on three sides and backed by the mountains. Its peculiar physical characteristcs have added a touch of maritime climate. It is neither too cold in winter, nor too hot in summer. The pleasant climate here has made the city an attractive holiday resort. That's why it is also called the "Switerland of the East".

游客：噢，我都有点眼馋了。

导游：I think you'll find yourself reluctant to leave.

游客：我想也是。

Section Ⅱ: Passage

可持续旅游

旅游在过去的几十年里呈现上升趋势，特别是在欧洲，短期国际旅行十分普遍。游客形形色色，消费水准不一，兴趣品味各异。各种各样的度假村、酒店应运而生，以满足他们的需要。例如，有些人喜欢简单的海滩度假，另一些人则偏爱更具特点的假期、安静的度假胜地、以家庭为核心的假期或者面向市场的利基目的地酒店。

随着技术的进步和诸如大飞机这样交通基础设施的完善，低成本航线以及更加便捷的机场使各种各样的旅游变得更加实惠。根据世卫组织2009年的估计，在任何特定的时间里，都会有50万左右的人在空中飞行。另外，人们的生活方式也有所改变。例如，一些达到退休年龄的人会一年四季在外旅游。这是网络销售旅游服务的结果。一些网站已经开始推出动态包价旅游项目，对于那些想走就走的游客提供专门的一价全包方案。

另一方面，随着旅游业的快速发展，越来越多的人关注旅游业对生态系统的负面影响。因此，出现了"可持续旅游"这个概念。"可持续旅游"指的是，参观某地时，想方设法只对环境、社会和经济产生积极影响。旅游涉及把游客送到目的地的主要交通、当地交通、住宿、娱乐、休闲和购物等。它可以与休闲旅游、商务旅游和"探亲访友"（VFR）旅游联系在一起。现在，人们广泛认识到，旅游开发应该是可持续的。

可持续旅游的设想是，力争这样管理所有资源，即在满足人们经济、社会和审美需求的同时，保持文化的完整性、重要的生态过程、生物多样性和生命支持系统。

可持续发展意味着，在满足当前需要的前提下，不损害子孙后代满足自己需要的能力。

可见，可持续旅游考虑到了生态和社会文化承载能力，包括让目的地的社区参与旅游发展规划等。它还包括整合旅游资源，适应当前的经济增长政策，减轻"大众旅游"给经济社会带来的负面影响。有人倡导在实现可持续旅游发展的过程中，从"生态的角度"去考虑"人"和"植物"。这与"积极推销"的做法和"经济"旅游规划完全相反。这两种做法都没有把旅游业发展对旅游目的地在生态学和社会学方面所带来的不利影响考虑在内。

Section Ⅲ: Passage

Cultural Heritage Tourism

Cultural heritage tourism, or just heritage tourism, is a branch of tourism oriented towards the cultural heritage of the location where tourism is occurring. The National Trust for Historic Preservation in the United States defines heritage tourism as "traveling to experience the places, artifacts and activities that authentically represent the stories and people of the past," and "heritage tourism can include cultural, historic and natural resources".

Culture has always been a major object of travel, as the development of the Grand Tour from the 16th century onwards attests. In the 20th century, some people have claimed, culture ceased to be the objective of tourism; tourism is now culture. Cultural attractions play an important role in tourism at all levels, from the global highlights of world culture to attractions that underpin local identities.

According to some experts, culture, heritage and the arts have long contributed to the appeal of tourist destination. However, in recent years "culture" has been rediscovered as an important marketing tool to attract those travelers with special interests in heritage and arts. In fact, cultural heritage tourism is the fastest growing segment of the tourism industry because there is a trend toward an increased specialization among tourists. This trend is evident in the rise in the volume of tourists who seek adventure, culture, history, archaeology and interaction with local people.

Cultural heritage tourism is important for various reasons. It has a positive economic and social impact, establishes and reinforces identity, helps preserve the cultural heritage, facilitates harmony and understanding among people, and supports culture and helps renew tourism. However, cultural heritage tourism can also create tensions and even conflict between the different stakeholders involved.

Cultural heritage tourism has a number of objectives that must be met within the context of sustainable development such as the conservation of cultural resources, accurate interpretation of resources, authentic visitor experience, and the increased revenues of cultural resources. We can see, therefore, that cultural heritage tourism is not only concerned with identification, management and protection of the heritage values but it must also be involved in understanding the impact of tourism on communities and regions, achieving economic and social benefits, providing financial resources for protection, as well as marketing and promotion. Heritage tourism involves visiting historical or industrial sites that may include old canals, railways, battlegrounds, etc. The overall purpose is to gain an appreciation of the past. It also refers to the marketing of a location to members of a diaspora who have distant family roots there.

附 录

口译对策

Coping Tactics

一、顺译方法

所谓顺译法，顾名思义就是按原句的顺序翻译。这与字对字的死译完全不同，其翻译单位是"意群"。顺译不仅是一种方法，更是一种原则，这是由口译的特点所决定的。口译的特点是即时性，口译人员没有充足的时间推敲琢磨。因此，为了提高效率，确保译文的口语化，减轻听众的负担，唯一的办法就是顺句驱动。

英汉两种语言在词序、语序上存在着较大的差异，因此，译员要根据意群及时"断句"。这一点与古代的"句读"颇有异曲同工之妙。实践中，可以根据自身的条件一个意群一个意群地翻译，也可以一两个意群连在一起翻译。一句话分成若干意群，然后通过句法手段、修辞手段连成一体，听上去自然地道。这就要求译者放弃以往笔译中颠倒语序重新组句的习惯，进行逆向思维。以下为例句。

（1）China is a developing country // with a population of 1.3 billion, // of whom 300 million are children under the age of 16, // making up about one fifth of the total number of children in the world.

中国是发展中国家，人口13亿，其中约3亿为16岁以下的儿童，约占世界儿童总数的1/5。

（2）We need to prepare for the negotiations now, // by taking a comprehensive approach // and injecting a sense of urgency, //if we are to bring them to a successful and early conclusion.

我们现在就需要为谈判作准备，要有全局观念，要有紧迫感，只有这样，才能尽快达成一致。

（3）China's membership of the WTO // is a good example // of how integrating it more fully into the international system // works to all of our advantage.

中国入世充分表明，中国全面融入国际社会对大家都有好处。

（4）The home and yard environment will also be improved // with the development of genetically-engineered lawns // that require fewer or no chemical treatments.

室内环境和庭院环境也将得到改善，这都得益于基因草坪的问世，这种草坪几乎不需要化学除草。

（5）In this most beautiful autumn season, // we welcome in Beijing the opening of the Fourth World Conference on Women, // the largest and one of the most important international meetings of its kind in world history.

在这个美丽的金秋时节，我们在北京迎来了第四届世界妇女大会的召开。这是世界史上规模最大、最为重要的国际会议之一。

(6) As Asia's world city, // Hong Kong is a widely acclaimed tourist destination // known for its international outlook, sophistication and diversity.

作为亚洲的一座世界级城市,香港是备受欢迎的旅游目的地,以其国际面貌和丰富多彩而闻名遐迩。

(7) 首先,请允许我//代表中国贸易代表团,并且以我个人名义,//对大家的盛情邀请和热情接待表示衷心的感谢,//对长期以来为促进中南经贸关系发展、增进中南人民友谊做出积极贡献的各界人士表示诚挚的敬意。

First of all, please allow me to express, on behalf of the Chinese trade delegation, and also in my own name, our profound gratitude for your kind invitation and gracious hospitality, and to send our greatest respects to all those who have made great contributions to the promotion of the development of China-South Africa trade relations and the friendship between our two peoples.

另外,还有一些常见的连词,在翻译时必须反其道而译之。如 before、after (following)、although 等应分别译成"之后""此前""不过"或者"但是"等。

(1) Work before pleasure.

这句话只能采取反译的方法,译成"工作在前,享乐在后"或者"工作第一,享乐第二"。

(2) Eat it before it gets cold.

这句话可以译成"趁热吃吧",也可以译成"吃吧,待会儿就凉了"。

(3) There are 10 minutes before we call it a day.

这句话根据不同情形可分别译成"10分钟后下班""10分钟后下课""10分钟后散会"以及"10分钟后结束"等。

(4) Look around before you come to my office.

先到处转转,然后到我办公室来。

(5) The meeting will resume at 3 p.m. after the Board of Trustees has met briefly.

会议下午3点继续,此前校董事会要碰个头。

(6) The Palestinians fired rockets into Israel following the Israeli bombing of West Bank and Gaza Strip.

巴勒斯坦人向以色列发射了火箭弹,此前,以色列轰炸了西岸和加沙地区。

(7) The deal will allow UN weapon inspectors' unconditional access to all suspected weapon sites. That includes 8 presidential palaces, although on those visits, diplomats will also have to be present.

该协议将允许联合国武器核查人员无条件进入所有被怀疑可能藏匿武器的地方,这包括8处总统官邸。不过(可是、但是、当然),对总统官邸进行核查时需要有外交官在场。

二、口译笔记

俗话说，好记性不如烂笔头。这句话在口译过程中显得尤为重要。由于口译现场时间紧，压力大，译者很难在有限的时间内记住全部信息。因此，为了保证信息的完整性和翻译的准确性，笔记便变得十分重要。

那么，笔记究竟记些什么呢？口译笔记，不同于一般速记，不求全，更不求细。一般而言，主要围绕"何人、何事、何时、何地、何由"五大方面来记录。此外，还包括数字、机构名称、技术术语等重要信息。

那么，如何做笔记呢？由于口译笔记只是补记忆之不足，且有"临时性"的特点，我们可以借助关键词、符号、图表等形式，把发言人的讲话重点、要点速记下来，以防遗漏。纸张要纵向分页，信息要阶梯式排列，这样条理清楚，重点突出。如果是站着工作，笔记本不宜过大，手掌大小最为合适。如果是坐着工作，有写字台，则大小纸张都可以，但最好不要超过 A4。另外，口译笔记宜少不宜多、宜精不宜粗。语言可以是目的语，也可以是源语，中间更是可以插入一些常见的符号或独创的符号。总之，只要能"激活"译者的记忆，什么方法都是好方法。

说到符号，常见的如下。

＜ 少于；不如；弱
＞ 多于；强
＝ 等于；相同；一样
≈ 近似；约等于；差不多
√ 准确；同意；支持
∴ 想
？问题；疑问
＆ 和；与
＋ 加上；优点
⊙ 国家；民族；人民
／与……的关系
♀ 女
↑ 上升；增加
↗ 渐增；改进；发展；加速
← 来自；源自；出发

≪ 远远少于；远不如
≫ 多得多；强得多
％ 百分比
× 错误；否定；不同意；禁止
≠ 不同；不等于
" 说；宣布；陈述
☆ 重要的
∥ 结束
－ 减去；弱点
⊕ 医院
∞ 总是
♂ 男
↓ 下降；减少
↘ 渐减；恶化；减速
→ 导致；结果；到达

常见的字母缩写如下。

e.g. 比如；例如
pol 政治
lib 自由的
gov't 政府

dept 部门
dem 民主
info 信息
intro 介绍、引入

bkgd 背景　　　　　　　　　　　bldg 大楼；建筑
cont'd 继续　　　　　　　　　　edu 教育
vs 反对　　　　　　　　　　　　ibid 同上
eco 经济

当然，每个人都可以根据自己的爱好、习惯，发明一套适合自己的速记方案。下面看几个实例。

（1）On the occasion of the Fifth International Fair for Investment and Trade, I would like to extend, on behalf of the Qingdao government, my warm welcome to our distinguished guests from all over the world.

5th int'l fair 4 invst & trad

I 4 QD gov't

wlcm 2 guests ← wrld

（2）"三农"工作进一步加强。中央财政用于"三农"的支出7253亿元，增长21.8%。大幅度提高粮食最低收购价。继续改善农村生产生活条件，农村饮水安全工程使6069万农民受益，新增510万沼气用户，新建和改造农村公路38万千米、农村电网线路26.6万千米，又有80万户农村危房得到改造，9.2万户游牧民实现了定居。

3 农 +

央财支 725.3 bln

21.8% ↑

+ + minim grain procure prix

↑ rural livin condi

H2o proj benef

60.69 mln

5.1 mln new 沼气 users

建 & 改 rd   38 万 km

pwr grid 26.6 万 km

80 万 危房 改

9.2 万户 nomads settld

（3）青岛大学与美国全球教育联盟联合举办的高等教育国际化研讨会今天正式开幕了。首先，我谨代表青岛大学对各位来宾和与会代表表示热烈欢迎，对迪克逊博士及各位美方朋友对此次联合会议的筹办所付出的巨大努力表示衷心感谢！

qdu ＋　GEA

hi'er ed. globl

guest ＋　reps 欢

dr. Dixon ＋　友　　努力　thx

(4) It is a real pleasure to be here to open the third meeting of our forum and to be welcoming such a distinguished and influential group of people from both our countries, many of whom are now old friends. The forum aims to represent the strength of the relationship between our two countries outside the political relationship and looking round today it is clear that the relationship is very strong indeed.

@ 主 3rd 4rum
欢 2 口 有识 人 ≫ 老友
strength / relation
x pol
strong

三、记忆训练

研究表明，人的记忆一般分为三种：瞬时记忆、短时记忆和长时记忆。

瞬时记忆只能使语言信息保持很短的时间，大约 0.25 秒至 2 秒，此后信息便会自动消失。瞬时记忆对于同声传译至关重要。可以毫不夸张地说，没有瞬时获取信息的能力，想做口译无异于异想天开。因此，瞬时记忆是口译的前提。

短时记忆，顾名思义，持续的时间较短，但比瞬时记忆要长。短时记忆的功能是把大脑捕捉到的信息暂时保存起来。然而，由于短时记忆很短，译者必须高度集中精神，调动所有因素，积极利用这些"暂存"的信息，进行两种语言之间的转化。可见，短时记忆是口译的关键。

长时记忆是人类获取知识的重要途径。没有长时记忆，人类的信息无法传递，知识无法传承。换言之，译员平时积累的东西越多，知识面越广，工作起来越有利，因为在口译过程中，是短时记忆和长时记忆共同作用才完成记忆工作的。所以，长时记忆是口译的基础。

既然记忆对于口译如此重要，那么，如何延长自己的短时记忆便成为口译成败的关键。一般来说，主要有以下几种方法。

（一）跟读练习

口译的基础是听懂原文，也就是要抓住信息。要想听懂原文，抓住关键的信息，重要的是要熟悉各种各样的"变体"，各种各样的口音。这就要求译员一开始要进行一段时间的跟读练习。跟读的目的不是简单地模仿，而是捕捉原文的大意，并进行复述。比如：

This city of 12 million seemed to be a good place to see how a National Geographic Magazine story is put together. Istanbul, a metropolis poised on both the European and Asian continents, lies right on the fault line that could rupture anytime. This city began sometime around 657 B. C. and has reinvented itself over and over throughout the centuries.

听完这一段文字后,译员的脑子里应出现一些重要的信息点：1200万人口、大都市、位于欧亚洲大陆之间、断裂线、公元前657年、今日变化等。之后,通过复述把它们连接起来,这样就达到了记忆的目的。

（二）逻辑记忆

口译的记忆训练和考试前填鸭式的突击背诵完全不同。口译的记忆训练是建立在逻辑的基础之上的。这样的记忆是连贯的,不是杂乱无章的。在这一阶段,译员仍然需要进行复述练习,通过逻辑,把原文大意"连接起来",形成一个有意义的整体。比如：

Sports help us learn cooperation. As the saying goes, there is no "I" in teamwork.

有人将此句译成"体育让人们学会合作精神。俗话说得好,在团队里没有'大写的我'"。该译文虽然字面上完全对等,但十分晦涩难懂。不难看出,Sports help us learn cooperation是中心句,为后面的文字定了调子。因此,按照逻辑关系,后面的一切都是围绕集体而不是个人展开的。故这里的I是"自我"的意思,因为"团队精神"讲究的是合作,而不是个人英雄主义。所以,后半句应译成"俗话说得好,在团队里没有'小我'"。可见,逻辑推理在锁定意义的同时,也有助于译员的记忆。

（三）形象记忆

形象记忆,也可以称之为记忆的视觉化,或视觉化记忆。图式理论认为,人的记忆可以以"图示"的方式呈现出来。也就是说,当译员听到一段文字之后,可以通过联想在大脑里构成一幅图画,这样能大大提高大脑的记忆功能。蓝天、大海、沙漠、草原给人们带来的是完全不同的视觉冲击。拿草原来说,它可能给人带来这样的画面或者想象：蓝蓝的天空、无垠的草地、成群的牛羊、清澈的河水、豪爽的牧民等。可见,形象记忆可在一定程度上减轻大脑的负担。

（四）情景记忆

情景记忆是学习语言的一个很好的途径,也是提高口译记忆力的一个很好的方法。比如,如果发言人讲的是与示威游行有关的内容,译员可以根据自身的经验、常识、知识,在大脑里反映出一系列特殊的词语或表达方式,如 take to the streets, riot police, tear gas, concussion grenade, club, baton, truncheon, water cannon, rubber bullet, violent clash, casualties, dead, injured, detained, arrested, detainees, sympathy strike, sympathy demonstration, curfew, martial law 等,并通过逻辑关系把它们连接起来,形成一个完整的语义链。

当然,口译的过程是三种记忆方式共同作用的结果,切莫厚此薄彼,将三者割裂开来。此外,每个人的先天条件不同,可根据自身的特点加强练习。

四、习语翻译

汉语习语包括成语、俗语、谚语、歇后语等。有些诗词名句由于长期使用，已经家喻户晓，也变成了习语的一部分。习语简洁有力，寓意深刻，其特殊的结构和美妙的节奏使之成为语言中一个非常重要的组成部分。然而，汉英两种语言由于文化的差异，其习语的特点也有不同。如何处理好习语的翻译，是口译成败的关键。

（一）套用

汉英两种语言中，有很多习语无论从意象还是从意义的角度来说都是完全对等的。翻译时可直接套用。如：

沧海一粟 a drop in the bucket

趁热打铁 Strike while the iron is hot.

百闻不如一见 Seeing is believing.

有其父必有其子 Like father, like son.

有志者事竟成 Where there is a will, there is a way.

种瓜得瓜，种豆得豆 As you sow, so you reap.

谋事在人，成事在天 Man proposes, Heaven disposes.

吃一堑，长一智 A fall into the pit, a gain in your wit.

嘴上无毛，办事不牢 A downy lip makes many a slip.

（二）借用

汉英两种语言中有一类习语，尽管意象不同，但意义完全相同。由于口译"即时"的特点，译者没有充足的时间去"诠释"习语中的意象。因此，借用现成的表达方式是一个便捷、聪明的处理方法。如：

不入虎穴，焉得虎子 No pains, no gains.

乌鸦笑猪黑 The pot calls the kettle black.

江山易改，本性难移 Can a leopard change its spots?

近朱者赤，近墨者黑 He who keeps company with the wolf will learn to howl.

巧妇难为无米之炊 One cannot make bricks without straw.

只要功夫深，铁杵磨成针 Constant dropping wears away a stone.

只许州官放火，不许百姓点灯 One man may steal a horse while another may not look over a hedge.

（三）节译

汉语习语中，有一种为并列结构，即前半部分和后半部分意思完全一样。翻译时只要译出其中一部分即可。否则，拖泥带水，不符合英语习惯。如：

高谈阔论 empty talk

贪官污吏 corrupt officials

装疯卖傻 play the fool
甜言蜜语 honeyed words
摇唇鼓舌 wag one's tongue
咬牙切齿 grind one's teeth

（四）释译

有时套用或借用习语会产生文化冲突，此时，最安全的办法是释译，即舍弃形象，只译意思。比如，如果将"智者千虑，必有一失"译成"Even Homer sometimes nods"，很容易产生歧义，故套用中性的成语或者采取释译的方法就比较可取。故该成语可译成"No man is wise at all times"。其他例子如下。

指鹿为马 talk black into white
塞翁失马，焉知非福 a blessing in disguise

（五）诗词翻译

诗词在许多重要的领导人的发言中层出不穷，比比皆是。引用诗词一方面显示发言人知识渊博，同时说明其重视听众的文化程度。因此，平时积累常用诗词名句的翻译就显得非常重要。以下引语均出自外国领导人来华演讲。

(1) Long distance separates no bosom friends.
海内存知己，天涯若比邻。

(2) Isn't it a delight to have friends from afar?
有朋自远方来，不亦乐乎？

(3) So many deeds cry out to be done, and always urgently; the world rolls on, times presses. Ten thousand years are too long, seize the day, seize the hour!
多少事，从来急；天地转，光阴迫。一万年太久，只争朝夕。

(4) Promise, I pray, that someday when the task done, we go back to farming. We'll surely rent a plot of ground and as pairing neighbors let us live.
险夷不变应尝胆，道义争担敢息肩。待得归农功满日，它年预卜买邻钱。

类似例子不胜枚举。由于口译现场操作的特点，译者不可能去考虑韵脚节奏等，只能译出大意。因此，唯一补救的方法就是未雨绸缪，加强平时的积累。

（六）力避"假朋友"

所谓假朋友是指字面意思相同而深层意思迥异的成语。比如，有人将"lock the stable door after the horse is stolen"译成"亡羊补牢"。从字面上看，非常对等。而实际上，二者的意思完全不同。"亡羊补牢"的寓意是"犹未为晚"。而英文成语却没有事后补救的意思。因此，"贼去关门"才是对等的翻译。再如，有人将"eat one's words"译成"食言"，而二者也仅仅是字面对等，其真实含义是"收回前言，承认错误"。"食言"的英语翻译应为"go back on one's word"。

五、词语精炼

英语中有句话，叫作"Brevity is the soul of wit"。汉语中有个成语，叫作"言简意赅"。二者表达的是同一个意思。这一观点在口译中尤为重要，这是因为口译受时间的限制，必须在最短的时间内把发言人的信息准确无误地传递出去。这就要求口译人员在平时多加练习，养成快速精炼的习惯。只有这样，才能在有限的时间内交出满意的答卷。

汉语因为节奏的原因，即"四字情结"，经常出现联合结构或者同义词堆砌的现象。此时，仅翻译一半即可（请参考习语翻译之"节译"）。如"跑冒滴漏"（leakage）、"铺天盖地"（overspread）、"南征北战"（fight on all fronts）、"东奔西走"（run around）、"男女老少"（men, women and children）、"夫妻老婆店"（mom-and-pop store）等。

有时为了加强语气，同义或近义的四字成语也常常叠用。对这类现象的处理方法依旧是"节译"。如"欣欣向荣、蒸蒸日上"（on the rise）、"班门弄斧、布鼓雷门"（teach fish to swim 或 teach a bird to sing 或 teach a spider to spin a web）等。

还有一种现象，如"多快好省"与"少慢差费"等。这种四字结构和前面的两种情况有所不同，每个组成部分都有独立的含义。按字面翻译，前者应译为"more, faster, better, and more economical"；而后者则应译成"fewer, slower, poorer and more costly"。然而，在口译现场，"时间就是一切"，谁赢得了时间，谁就赢得了胜利，谁就能出色地完成任务。因此，可以考虑将它们分别译成 cost-effectively 和 inefficiently。

汉语中很多表达方式本身就是一种"缩略语"，如"三从四德""三纲五常"等。它们本身有着丰富的含义。如果是笔译，我们完全可以采取脚注、尾注和内注的方式进行处理。

（1）"三从四德"可译为：

a. the three types of obedience and four virtues

b. three types of obedience (in ancient China a woman was required to obey her father before marriage, and her husband during married life and her sons in widowhood) and four virtues (fidelity, physical charm, propriety in speech and efficiency in needle work)

（2）"三纲五常"可以译为：

a. the three cardinal guides and the five constant virtues as specified in the feudal ethical code

b. the Three Cardinal Guides (ruler guides subject, father guides son and husband guides wife) and Five Constant Virtues (benevolence, righteousness, propriety, knowledge and sincerity)

试想一下，如果在口译（尤其是同声传译）现场采取上述翻译方法，结果会如何？因此，为了抢时间，抓要点，可以灵活处理成 wifely submission and virtue 和 principle of feudal moral conduct。

同样，很多政治词语的翻译也可借鉴以上方法。如"八荣八耻"可精炼为 socialist concept of honor and disgrace，而"五讲四美三热爱"可提炼为 socialist moral standards。

其他的例子如：

全心全意 wholeheartedly　　　无法无天 unruly
三心二意 half-hearted　　　　五湖四海 everywhere
老弱病残 the infirm　　　　　五颜六色 colorful
形形色色 all sorts of　　　　　林林总总 numerous

类似的例子，不胜枚举。关键是平时要善于积累，方可厚积薄发。

六、文化翻译

各个民族由于生存环境的不同，形成了迥异的文化及特殊的表达方式。因此，翻译时，必须考虑文化因素。否则，即使字面意思"相等"，也难以达意，甚至会南辕北辙。比如，intellectual 一词，字典释义为"知识分子"。其实，不是每一个受过教育的人都是 intellectual。在英语中，能够称得上的 intellectual 的人并不多，因为该词的真正含义是"高级知识分子"。因此，翻译时，切忌对号入座，望文生义。

（一）称呼上的差异

很多人将"这位是王厂长"译成"This is Director Wang"。乍一看完全对等，然而，不符合英语习惯。正确的翻译应为"This is Mr. Wang, our director"。这是因为英语中能够用头衔加姓直接称呼对方的表达方式并不多。常见的无非是 president、governor、mayor、judge、professor、Dr. 等。再如，"夫人"一词，在日常英语中可以译为 ma'am 或者 Mrs.，如 Mrs. White（怀特夫人）。然而，在正式场合，如国际会议上，"夫人"这个称呼并非 Mrs. 一词就可以完全解决的。也就是说，在很多情况下，Mrs. 就显得无能为力了。试比较下列说法。

(1) 尼克松总统和夫人　Mr. President and Mrs. Nixon
(2) 史密斯博士和夫人　Dr. and Mrs. Smith
(3) 大使先生和夫人　Mr. Ambassador and Madame

在例（1）和例（2）中，都出现了姓氏，故译为 Mrs.。然而，在例（3）中没有出现姓氏，故译为 Madame。Madame 是尊称，如 Madame Curie（居里夫人）和 Madame Soong Ching Ling（宋庆龄夫人）等。

另外，"Dear Chinese friends""Dear Governor"中的 dear 不能想当然地译为"亲爱的"，而应根据汉语习惯译为"尊敬的"。

（二）问候语的差别

问候语是人际关系的"润滑油"。准确译好问候语常常是译文成功的关键。如，将"一路辛苦了"译成"You must be tired"或"You must have a tiring journey"纯属死译。这不但无法达意，反而可能引起反感。正确的译法应为"How's your trip?""Did you have a nice flight?"或者"Did you have a good journey?"。

再如，中国人见面一般会问三句话，"贵姓？""贵庚？"以及"在哪里高就？"。第一句话没有问题。第二句话在西方人眼里是禁忌，对女性来说尤其如此。因此，一般来说是不会问的。第三句话"在哪里高就？"初次见面时一般也很少有人问起。一定要问，也不能简单地将其译成"What's your job?"或者"What's your occupation?"这两种译法虽然字面对等，但不符合文化习惯，因为很多西方人没有固定的职业，直接发问的结果可能令对方尴尬。因此，比较得体的译法应为"What do you do for a living?"。

（三）套话的翻译

和问候语一样，套话的翻译必须符合习惯用法，否则，直译、死译、硬译必定会让人觉得生硬、死板，有时甚至会造成误解。比如：

(1) 请大家多提宝贵意见。

如果将这句话译为"Your valuable suggestions, advice and criticism are always welcome / appreciated"或者"Please give us your valuable comments"，其结果只能是冷场。换言之，没有任何人会开口说话，因为谁也不知道自己的意见是否"宝贵"。因此，地道的翻译是将上述两个译文中的 valuable 一词去掉。

(2) 今天的菜不好，请多多包涵。

中国人的特点是自谦。遇到类似表达方式绝对不可直译，否则给以虚伪的感觉。因此，如果是用餐开始时讲的，可译为"Bon appetite"或者"Please enjoy"；如果是用餐完毕时说的，则应译成"I hope you have enjoyed it"。

(3) 讲得不好，请各位多多原谅。

这也是一句自谦的说法。如果直译，给听众以"不诚实"甚至是"蔑视"的感觉。因此，可以参照西方人的习惯，直接译成"Thank you for your attention（time）"。反过来，如果将英语发言人的结束语"Thank you for your attention（time）"直译成"谢谢大家的听讲"或者"谢谢大家的时间"，也显得生硬拗口，而且也不地道。所以，应根据汉语的习惯，简单译成"谢谢大家"即可。

(4) 三句话。

"三句话"是很多身居要职的人的开场白，笔者在一次大型国际会议上就亲历了这一幕。当时，翻译简单地译成"Three sentences"。不料，发言人滔滔不绝，洋洋洒洒，岂止 30 句！场面好不尴尬。其实，碰到类似情况，根据具体情形完全可以灵活处理，如"I want to say/add a few words（about…）; I'd like to make a few remarks; Let me say a few words first; Now allow me to say a few words;

Let me just try to summarize here"等。

（5）姜还是老的辣。

国人常用这句话来恭维年长的人。一般情况下，可译成"Older and wiser" "The older the wiser"等。如果对方确系老人，当他说"I'm getting old. I am falling apart"时，你不妨说，"Old is good; The older, the wiser"，或者更客气一点说"The more senior, the wiser"。与国人喜欢论资排辈不同，西方人不愿意当"老大"，也就是说，不愿意说老，因为"老"总是和健康欠佳、机能减退等联系在一起。所以，当西方人碰到七八十岁的老人不得不问年龄时，他们会很诙谐地问道"How young are you?"，祝寿时会说"Oh, you are seventy-eight years young"。国人喜欢在姓前加"老"或者"小"以示亲切。国内的英语课本里，有的也相应地译成 Old Wang、Xiao Li。这些自以为清楚明白的中式英语到了英语里则变得不伦不类，非驴非马，不但无法达意，还容易引起误解。因此，我们不妨借助语言中的一种修辞现象委婉语来表达。比如"残疾人"，不要说 a disabled / crippled / handicapped person，而要说 a physically-challenged person 或者干脆说 a challenged person；"矮人"不是 a short person，而是 a vertically-challenged person；"胖人"不是 a fat person，而是 a horizontally-challenged person；"长相欠佳"不是 ugly，而是 visually-challenged；"单身、孤单"不是 lonely，而是 relationship-challenged；"经济不宽裕"不是 poor，而是 financially challenged。再如，"老人"在英语里不说 old people，而要说 senior adult，mature person，seasoned citizen 或者 golden-ager，以示尊重。

（6）小小礼物，不成敬意，还望笑纳。

国人的最大特点是在外人面前"自谦"，而这在外事活动中构成了翻译的一道屏障。比如上面这句话，如果直译，则成了"This humble gift is not good enough to show my respect to you. I hope you will kindly take it"。结果如何呢？结果老外会满脸不悦，甚至觉得国人虚伪。明知不好，干吗送我呀？打发要饭的吗？这么好的东西还说不好，这不是虚伪吗？是不是要我感恩戴德呢？看，好事变成了坏事。其实，英语中有很多说法。最常见的是"Here's a little something for you. I hope you like it"。

（7）都在酒里了。

"都在酒里了"这句话是宴会期间最常见的一句话，在生意酒会上更是屡见不鲜。有人曾把它译为"We are all in the wine"。稍微有点常识的人都知道：一、这是不可能的。人怎么可能在酒里？二、国人喜欢泡药酒，里面蛇、乌龟什么都有。这样说，不是等于变相骂人吗？笔者在一家西餐馆用餐时，偶然看见一个烟灰缸上有三个英语单词"says it all"。一看才知，这些烟灰缸是一家咖啡经营商送的，可见是该咖啡的广告用语。咖啡可以用，酒为什么不可以呢？所以，当一个人举起酒杯为客人敬酒、口里说着"都在酒里了"时，不妨译成"It says it all"。此处的 it 当然指的是手里的酒。

（四）文化词的翻译

所谓文化词，指的是一种语言中特有的现象，包括风土人情、文化人物、历史事件等。由于口译自身的特点，译者不可能像笔译那样通过脚注或尾注的方式进行解释。因此，"内注"便成了译者的不二选择。不过，加内注时应注意做到言简意赅，切忌拖泥带水，喧宾夺主。内注得当会起到画龙点睛的作用。以下例句译文中的斜体部分均为内部注释。

（1）我喜欢太极，也喜欢武术。

I love Taiji, *or shadow boxing*, and wushu, *or martial arts* as well.

（2）四合院是北京的一大特色。

Siheyuan, *or courtyard buildings*, are part of Beijing.

（3）过端午节的时候，人们都吃粽子。

People eat zongzi, *a pyramid-shaped dumpling made of glutinous rice in bamboo or reed leaves*, during the Dragon-boat Festival.

（4）我去年参观过秦始皇陵。

Last year I visited the Mausoleum of Qinshihuang, *the first emperor of China*.

七、变词为句

英语中很多词或短语在翻译的时候可以根据汉语的习惯单独成句，或者成为独立成分。这种技巧常用于以下几种情形。

1. 现在分词、过去分词或分词短语用作定语或悬垂结构时，如 licensed and metered, crushing, as expected 等。

（1）Licensed and metered, all the taxis in the city provide good services.

该市所有的出租车都有运营执照，都安装了计价器，为客人提供优质服务。

（2）If non-performing loans reach the same level in Thailand, they will be a crushing 45% of GDP.

如果泰国的不良贷款达到相同水平，将占 GDP 总额的 45%，那对泰国经济来说将是致命一击。

（3）As expected, President Bush has signed a war spending bill. It was a bipartisan effort that seems to have left both Democrats and Republicans unhappy.

果然不出所料，布什总统签署了军费支出议案。这是两党共同努力的结果，然而，民主党和共和党对此似乎都不满意。

（4）Qingdao, known as Switzerland in the East, is a beautiful coastal city.

青岛素有东方瑞士之称，是一座美丽的海滨城市。

2. 一些表达态度、看法的副词，如 arguably, undoubtedly, conspicuously,

obviously，incredibly，incidentally，sure enough，correctly 等。

（1）John is arguably the greatest captain in Chelsea's history already and I am certain he will do a fantastic job for England.

可以说，约翰是切尔西历史上最伟大的队长。我相信，在英格兰队他一定也会干得非常漂亮。

（2）Translating methods are undoubtedly the core problems we are confronted with in translation.

毫无疑问，翻译方法是翻译过程中所面临的核心问题。

（3）Women were conspicuously absent from the planning committee.

引人注意的是，规划委员会里没有一名女性委员。

（4）He obviously needed a wife.

显然，他需要成家了。

（5）He has an incredibly sharp memory.

他记忆力超群，令人难以置信。

（6）Dr. Watson，incidentally，was American-born，which shows that basic science is international.

顺便说一句，华生博士出生于美国，这表明基础科学具有国际性。

（7）Sure enough，the people of Israel are to be found everywhere today.

毫无疑问，当今以色列人在世界各地随处可见。

（8）Everywhere，you sense—correctly—that Cape Town is South Africa's most famous city.

无论在什么地方，你都会感到开普敦是南非最有名的城市。这种感觉是千真万确的。

3. 某些同位语表达成分，如 the capital city of Shandong Province，home to more than twenty ethnic groups 等。

（1）Jinan，the capital city of Shandong Province，is famous for its springs.

济南是山东省政府所在地，因泉水而闻名。

（2）Home to more than twenty ethnic groups，Yunnan Province lies in the south of China and abounds in fruits.

云南省是 20 多个少数民族的故乡，它位于中国南部，盛产水果。

4. 其他由 as，one of the many，one of the most 构成的特殊结构，如：

（1）The city government plans to divert 10 million yuan into preventing its youths from using drugs，as part of the city's drug control program.

该市计划拨款 1000 万元，防止青少年吸毒，这是该市禁毒计划的一部分。

（2）I rented a bike at one of the many shops which cost me a few dollars a day.

这里有很多自行车租赁店铺。我在其中一家租了一辆,每天的租金只有几美元。

八、数字翻译

数字翻译是口译中的一大重点,也是一大难点。说它是重点,是因为数字传递着重要的信息。说它是难点,是因为英汉两种语言在数字表达方式上不尽相同,或者说差异很大。这就要求译员平时要掌握规律,加强练习,从而达到融会贯通、游刃有余的地步。

(一) 具体数字的翻译

1. 汉语的数字是以"十"的倍数来表示的,即个、十、百、千、万、十万、百万、千万、亿、十亿、百亿、千亿、万亿等,而英语的数字在"千"以内与汉语相同。

个 = one
十 = ten
百 = hundred
千 = thousand

在超过"千"以后,以"千"的倍数来表示。

一万 = ten thousand(十个千)
十万 = hundred thousand(百个千)

"百万"有对等的表达方式,million;"百万"以上的数字则用"百万"的倍数来表示。

千万 = ten million(十个百万)
亿 = hundred million(百个百万)

"十亿"有对等的表达方式,billion;"十亿"以上的数字则用"十亿"的倍数来表示。

百亿 = ten billion
千亿 = hundred billion

"万亿"(又叫"兆")有对等的表达方式,trillion。

2. 百万以上的数字,最简便的方法是把"百万"以后的数字用"点"(即.)多少来表示。

960 万 = 9.6 million
8888 万 = 88.88 million

3. 如前所述,"亿"是一百个百万,因此,

567,890,000 = 567.89 million

4. 十亿以上的数字,最简便的方法是把"十亿"以后的数字用"点"(即.)多少来表示。

13 亿 = 1.3 billion
168 亿 = 16.8 billion
1234 亿 = 123.4 billion

5.万亿是 trillion，因此，万亿以后的数字，最简便的方法是把"万亿"以后的数字用"点"（即.）多少来表示。

56789 亿 = 5.6789 trillion

（二）非具体数字的翻译

所谓非具体数字的翻译，主要指的是一些笼统的数字。这些"数字"在日常生活中使用频率很高，需要熟练掌握。如：

几（若干）several, a few, some

十几 more than ten, over ten, no more than twenty, ten-odd（a ten-odd committee）

几十 dozens of

数以百计 hundreds of

数以千计 thousands of

数以万计 tens of thousands of

数十万 hundreds of thousands of

数百万 millions of

数千万 tens of millions of

亿万 hundreds of millions of

（三）具体数字的记录方法

由于数字本身的重要性及其特殊性，有人总结出了"点三杠四"和"缺位补零"的记录方法。所谓"点三杠四"，或者"三位一点、四位一竖"，具体而言，就是"英文数字是三位一节，汉语数字是四位一节"。前者从右往左分别对应的是 thousand、million、billion 等，后者从右而左分别对应的是"万""亿"等。如：

one hundred twenty three million four hundred fifty six thousand seven hundred eighty nine

记录1：123m 456 th 789

记录2：1 | 2345 | 6789

记录1将声音准确记录下来。记录2根据汉语四位一节的特点自右而左标记出来，可以迅速准确读出数字为"一亿两千三百四十五万六千七百八十九"。再如：

八千七百六十五万四千三百二十一

记录1：8765 万 4321

记录2：87,654,321

记录1将声音准确记录下来。记录2根据英语三位一节的特点自右而左标记出来，可以迅速准确读出数字为 eighty-seven million six hundred fifty-four thousand three hundred twenty-one。

有时，数字中出现空位现象，如 fifty-four thousand and eighty-one，需要"缺位补零"。

记录 1：54th 81

记录 2：5 ∣ 4081

记录 1 中"零"没有体现出来。因此，为了准确，在翻译前需要像记录 2 一样把"零"补上。

汉译英也是一样的，如"八万六百四十五"可以标记如下。

记录 1：8 万 645

记录 2：80，645

同样，记录 1 中"零"没有体现出来。记录 2 补零以后，很容易就可以读出来。

九、词类转换

美国著名翻译理论家尤金·奈达说过，翻译是翻译意思。换言之，翻译不是简单的词语对等，也不是对原文结构的临摹。因此，在实际翻译过程中，应根据译入语的需要，进行词类转换。如：

(1) 他烧得一手好菜。

He's a great cook.

(2) 她晕船。

She's a bad sailor.

(3) This is a booklet on the details about our department.

这里有一本小册子，详细介绍了我系的情况。

(4) I'm sorry he's out at the moment.

很抱歉，他此刻不在。

从以上例句中不难看出，译文均从某种意义上进行了词类转换。也只有这样，才能使译文地道通顺。这里着重介绍英译汉时经常出现的词类转换情况。

(一) 介词转换成动词

(1) I'm all for it.

我举双手赞成。

(2) All peace-loving people are strongly against arms race.

一切爱好和平的人们都强烈反对军备竞赛。

(二) 名词转化成动词

(1) The sight of the snake made his hair stand on end.

一看到蛇，他便毛发倒竖，头皮发麻。

(2) The little girl pales at the mere mention of dogs.

一提到狗，小女孩吓得脸都白了。

(3) As a result, importance is attached to the inculcation and accumulation of knowledge, respect to authority, cultivation of students' rigor and preciseness in learning.

因而，（中国教育）注重传授和积累知识，尊重权威，培养学生的严谨学风。

(4) Reflections of the new system are different.

对新体制，人们反响不一。

(三) 副词转化成动词

(1) He wasn't in when you called.

你来电话的时候，他出去了。

(2) Five days later, the patient was up and about again.

5天后，病人又开始下地走动了。

(四) 形容词转化成动词

(1) She was asleep the whole day.

她睡了整整1天。

(2) Mary was sure that she had given the book to Tom.

玛丽肯定自己把书给了汤姆。

(五) 名词转换成形容词

(1) Insecurity and turbulence appear all-pervasive.

举国上下，危机四伏，动荡不安。

(2) The plan was a complete success.

计划非常成功。

(六) 形容词转变为副词

(1) The plane landed safe.

飞机安全着陆。

(2) That's sheer nonsense.

那纯粹是一派胡言。

(七) 副词转换成形容词

(1) Traditionally, the two countries had good relations.

两国一直保持着传统友谊。

(2) They had fully prepared for the exam.

他们为考试做好了充分准备。

(八) 副词转换成名词

(1) Physically weak as he was, he worked very hard.

他尽管身体虚弱，但工作非常卖力。

(2) He is a mentally sound man, though.

尽管如此，他依然是一个思想健康的人。

（九）形容词转变成名词

(1) He was a very eloquent speaker.

他口才很好。

(2) The rich should not look down upon the poor.

富人不该看不起穷人。

其实，在翻译实践中还有很多种类型的词类转换。关键是译者要着眼于译入语的行文习惯，灵活处理。汉译英时也不例外，应根据英语的行文习惯，酌情处理。

十、词语省略

有人认为，汉语是文学的语言，英语是科学的语言，这种说法不无道理。这是因为汉语靠意思连贯（意合），英语靠句法成句（形合）。也就是说，除个别情况外，英语句子的句法形式与功能必须是完整的。例如，含有及物动词的句子，必须有主语、谓语和宾语，缺一不可。

无论是汉语也好，英语也罢，在翻译时都必须根据译入语的习惯进行增减。所谓省略，是删去一些可有可无的词，绝不是任意删减，更不是删去原文的信息内容。

从汉译英的角度来看，省略重点有三大类。

（一）省略表示范畴的词语

汉语中的一些范畴词，如"问题、现象、状态、面貌、事业、制度、局面、情况、工作、任务"等，本身没有实质意义，翻译时可以省去不译。如：

(1) 新中国成立以来，尤其是改革开放后，我国的经济发展取得了举世瞩目的成就，但贫困问题依旧是当前不可回避的一个现实问题。

Since the founding of the People's Republic of China, and especially since reform and opening-up, great achievements have been made in China's economic development. However, poverty is inevitably a serious problem.

(2) 市政府正在采取积极措施解决失业问题。

The municipal government is taking active measures to deal with unemployment.

(3) 本文介绍了中国的人口状况。

The essay touches upon the population in China.

(4) 出现紧急情况，请走楼梯。

In case of an emergency, please use the stairs.

(5)《联合国气候变化框架公约》及其《京都议定书》凝聚了各方的广泛共识，是国际合作应对气候变化的法律基础和行动指南。

The United Nations Framework Convention on Climate Change and the Kyoto Protocol reflect the broad consensus among all parties and serve as the legal basis and guide for international cooperation on climate change.

（6）中国人民的面貌、社会主义中国的面貌发生了历史性变化。

Historic changes have taken place in the Chinese people and socialist China.

（二）省略原文中重复出现的词语

汉语不怕重复，然而，这却是英语行文的大忌。因此，翻译时，原文中重复出现的词语可使用代词替代，或干脆省略不译。如：

（1）长征是历史纪录上的第一次，长征是宣言书，长征是宣传队，长征是播种机。

The Long March is the first of its kind in the annals of history. It is a manifesto, a propaganda force and a seeding-machine.

（2）全国社会稳定，政治稳定，处处呈现出生机勃勃的景象。

Social and political stability throughout the country makes for a vibrant outlook.

（三）省略修饰语

汉语中有很多修饰语，主要为副词和形容词。其作用是加强语气，如"隆重庆祝""正式开幕""胜利闭幕""欢聚一堂"等。翻译成英语时可直接省略。如：

（1）我宣布第20届洛阳牡丹花会正式开幕。

I declare the opening of the twentieth Luoyang Peony Festival.

（2）今天，我们在这里欢聚一堂，热烈欢迎史密斯先生。

We are here today to give Mr. Smith a warm welcome.

（3）今天，我们在这里集会，隆重庆祝中华人民共和国成立60周年。

We are gathered together here today to celebrate the 60th anniversary of the founding of the People's Republic of China.

（4）遏制气候变暖，拯救地球家园，是全人类共同的使命。

It is the common mission of the entire mankind to curb global warming and save our planet.

从英译汉的角度来看，省略的种类较多，如冠词、代词、人称代词、非人称代词、物主代词、并列连词、从属连词、介词、重复词、修饰语等。

（四）省略从属连词、关系代词/副词

汉语中的逻辑关系往往隐含在句子中，由语序加以体现。因此，有时可以省略英语中一些表示原因、条件或时间的从属连词，以及关系从句中的关系代词/副词。如：

（1）I can't go now because I'm very busy.

我很忙，这会儿去不了。

（2）If I had known it, I wouldn't have done that.

早知如此，绝对不会那么做。

（3）When I turned round, I saw her running toward me.

我转过身来，看见她正朝我跑来。

（4）She wept as she spoke.

她边说边哭。

（5）When a certain species is affected by our chemicals, entire food chains are disrupted.

某一物种受到化学物质的影响，会导致整个食物链的失衡。

（6）This sets off a chain reaction where the permanent changes in weather bring calamities such as the rise to diseases that once could not thrive in cold climates, the destruction of specific ecosystems, desertification and unpredictable weather.

这引起了连锁反应，气候的恒久变化引发灾难。例如，以前在寒冷地带鲜见的某些疾病的发病率上升，对特殊物种生态系统的破坏，土壤荒漠化以及变幻无常的气候。

（五）以信息对等为基础，译语的略译处理

这主要是由译语的行文习惯决定的，省略后既保留了原语的信息，又使译语简洁、自然、地道。如：

（1）And the experts agree it will take a couple of weeks for everyone to get used to his or her own bed, and that it will get worse before it gets better, but success can be achieved.

专家一致认为，大家需要几周的时间才能适应自己的床，而且情况会暂时变得更糟，不过终究会成功的。

（2）Our emissions of sulfur and nitrogen produce a phenomenon called acid rain, which is harmful to plants and animals that live in the water.

硫黄和氮气的排放，造成了酸雨现象，危及水生动植物。

（3）应对气候变化必须在可持续发展的框架下统筹安排，决不能以延续发展中国家的贫穷和落后为代价。

Action on climate change must be taken within the framework of sustainable development and should by no means compromise the efforts of developing countries to get rid of poverty and backwardness.

为达到加强语气或表达优美的目的，汉语经常使用结构对称而信息重叠的表达，英译时可略译。如：

（1）近朱者赤，近墨者黑。

Touch pitch and you will be defiled.

（2）聚精会神搞建设，一心一意谋发展

concentrate on development

(3) 吸纳百家优长，兼集八方精义

call for drawing upon the strength of others

十一、词语增补

前面说过，汉语是意合的语言，英语是形合的语言。因此，汉译英时，增补便成了必不可少的手段。

(一) 增补主语

汉语中的无主句在翻译时必须补出"所谓的"主语。在下面的例子中，斜体部分为增补部分，否则，不符合英语的行文习惯。如：

(1) 下雨了。

It is raining.

(2) 8 点了。起床吧，懒鬼。

It's eight o'clock. Get up, you lazybones.

(二) 增补连接词

汉语，尤其是口语中，在很多场合都省略连词。译成英语时，需要根据情况增补。如：

(1) 你去我就去。否则，我宁愿待在家里。

I'll go if you are going. If not, I'd rather stay at home.

(2) 昨晚下雨了，今早地都湿了。

It rained last night, for the ground is wet this morning.

(三) 根据语境、事实、逻辑关系等因素增补适当的词语

(1) 她起床后，穿好衣服，直接奔往灾区。

She got up, put on her clothes, and made straight for the disaster area.

(2) 大连是一个经济发达的沿海开放城市。

Dalian is a coastal city with a fairly developed economy.

(3) 我们的使命就是要全面建设小康社会。

Our mission is to build a moderately well-off society in an all-round way.

(4) 青岛在轻纺方面有着传统优势。

Qingdao enjoys traditional strengths in textile and other light industries.

(5) 我们的周边国家和地区纷纷以较低的价格吸引客户。

Some manufacturers from our neighboring countries and regions have attracted the customers with lower prices.

(6) 联合国项目

UN-sponsored programs

(7) 美元资产

US dollar-denominated assets

英语通常非常简洁，言简意赅。然而，如果逐字逐句翻译过来总觉得意犹未尽，行文欠妥。此时，增补就变得十分必要。

1. 在下面的例子中，如果没有括号里的文字，便不符合汉语习惯。如：

(1) The global economy is a fact.

经济全球化是个（不争的）事实。

(2) Throughout my term as Secretary-General, I have sought to place human beings at the center of everything we do — from conflict prevention to development to human rights.

在我担任秘书长期间，我总是坚持以人为本的方针，从预防冲突到（谋求）发展，（再）到（维护）人权，（无不如此）。

(3) Thank you for your invitation and hospitality.

感谢您的（盛情）邀请和（热情）款待。

(4) Education in Britain is compulsory. All children must go to school from the age of five to sixteen. That's the law.

英国实行义务教育。5 至 16 岁的孩子都必须上学。这是法律（规定的）。

(5) Thanks you for your words of welcome.

感谢您（热情洋溢）的欢迎词。

(6) Welcome to Qingdao-The Island City.

欢迎到青岛来。（欢迎到）"岛城"（来）。

2. 很多抽象名词在翻译时需要增补适当的词语。如：

(1) They were busy making final preparations for the exam.

他们正在为考试做着最后的准备（工作）。

(2) UNAIDS Executive Director Peter Piot said that in the world who are still widespread poverty, many of the hungry, grain prices soaring and food shortage is a serious threat to the fight against AIDS.

联合国艾滋病规划署执行主任彼得·皮奥特说，在世界上那些贫困（现象）仍很普遍、饥民众多的地区，粮价飞涨和食品供应不足正严重威胁着抗击艾滋病行动。

(3) The crew members were able to deal with all kinds of emergencies.

机组成员可以应付任何紧急（情况）。

(4) Despite the pressure from the interest groups, the Obama Administration publicly urged an easing of tensions with Iran.

顶着利益集团的巨大压力，奥巴马政府公开主张缓和同伊朗的紧张（关系）。

十二、语境定义

英文中有一句名言,叫作"词本无意,意由境生"(No context, no text),足见上下文在阅读乃至翻译中的重要作用。比如 Time flies,一看到这句话,大多数人会不约而同地将其译成"时间飞逝"。其实,离开了上下文,很难说这是一个正确的翻译,因为这句话至少还有另外一个意思,那就是"测一下苍蝇的飞行速度"。以下例句都离不开上下文,必须在特定的语境中获取其特殊的含义。

(1) The dog had an accident on the rug.

accident 最常见的意思是"事故"。如果将其译成"狗在地毯上出事故了",比较令人费解。这里,on the rug 排除了 accident 作为"事故"解的意思。也正是因为 on the rug 这个特殊的语境,该句的正确译文应为"狗拉在地毯上了"。

(2) Surprise Attack on Pearl Harbor

著名的珍珠港事件改变了太平洋战争的态势,为人们留下了无尽的思考。然而,Surprise Attack on Pearl Harbor 究竟应如何翻译?这主要取决于作者的身份及立场。如果作者是美国人,且是珍珠港事件的幸存者,那么,应毫不犹豫地译成"偷袭珍珠港"。但是,也有文献不这么翻译,而是字面上略作改动,译作"奇袭珍珠港"。一字之差,情感含义天壤之别。

(3) The party was over. Everybody was longing for a horizontal position.

有人将此句译成"晚会结束了,每个人都渴望一种水平位置"。译文给人以不知所云的感觉。何为"水平位置"?其实,结合"晚会结束了"这句话不难看出,a horizontal position 是"躺下来休息"的意思,因为大家都玩累了。因此,正确的译文应为,"晚会结束了,大家都想躺下来休息休息"。

(4) The small boat disappeared into the horizon.

有人将这句话译成"小船消失在地平线上"。horizon 可以表示"地平线",也可以表示"海平面"。"地平线"是天地交接的地方。所以,船无论如何也不可能消失在"地平线"上。因此,该句应译成"小船消失在水天相接的地方"。

(5) The Memorandum of Understanding was signed in May by the Corporation of London and the Shanghai Municipality.

本句的焦点在于 corporation 一词。该词最常见的意思是"公司"。如果认为谅解备忘录是由伦敦公司和上海市政府签署的,有悖于常识。根据上下文以及外交对等的原则,the Corporation of London 应为"伦敦市政府"。

(6) Britain is a whole-hearted supporter of free trade since the Gatt's establishment. We remain an unashamed champion of free trade today.

champion 有"冠军、勇士、战士、捍卫者、保护者、支持者"等意思。本例的前一句是"自关贸总协定成立以来,英国一直是自由贸易忠实的支持者"。根据该句构成的语境,champion 的意思不言自明,应该是"倡导者、捍卫者"。所以,第二句应译为"如今，我们依然是自由贸易公开的捍卫者。"

（7）A：I got a ticket yesterday.

B：Welcome to the club.

译文：A：我昨天收到一张罚单。

B：欢迎来到俱乐部。

这种译文读后让人如堕五里雾中。收到罚单与俱乐部之间有什么关系？根据语境，我们知道，第二句话的意思应是"同病相怜""同是天涯沦落人"之意，因此应该译为"我也一样啊！"或者"我们是难兄难弟啊！"。

下列例子都与 killer 有关。由于搭配不同，其含义也不同。

（8）He's got a killer smile.

The green skirt is a real killer.

The English exam was a real killer.

killer 原意为"杀手"，并由此衍生出很多意思。根据不同的搭配，三句话的意思分别是：

他的微笑很迷人。

那件绿裙子真好看。

英语考试难得不得了。

下列例句的翻译都与金融危机的语境相关。

（9）Comparing economic statistics is inevitably a "glass is half empty" versus "glass is half full" kind of game. Both Pollyannas and Cassandras can marshal endless statistics to support their version of events.

对比经济数据不可避免地成了"杯子半空"对"杯子半满"式的游戏，乐观和悲观的经济预言家们都可无休止地列举数据，用以支持各自的观点。

（10）Uncertainty means that it is reasonable to pull your horns in a bit—and diversify away from stocks, emphasizing a diverse group of assets that are less correlated to the stock market.

经济的不确定性意味着应适当限制投资行为，应规避股票，使资产投资多样化，并尽量不涉及股市。

（11）The top hedge managers I know are more focused on playing defense until the dust settles.

我认识的高层对冲基金经理更注重规避风险，谨慎行事，静待经济恢复正常。

十三、长句处理

总的来说，汉语中短句居多，而英语则以长句见长。英译汉时，如果句子过长，一方面不符合汉语习惯，另一方面会给译者增加负担，同时也给听众增加压力。因此，必须对其进行"切割"处理，即断句。断句的前提是"意群"，而切割后如何衔接是口译成败的关键。

造成英译汉句子冗长的主要原因在于译者不知断句，定语过长。初学者往往死译原文结构，且前后颠倒，结果译文拖沓，逻辑不清，影响理解。因此，如何处理好原文较长的定语/同位语或定语/同位语从句，如何做到化整为零，是对口译人员顺译能力的一大考验。如：

(1) The notion that the source of East Asia's rapid economic growth has permanently dried up is simply wrong. (同位语从句)

译文一：那种认为东亚经济快速增长的源头已经彻底枯竭的想法是完全错误的。

译文二：有人认为，东亚经济快速增长的源头已经彻底枯竭，这种想法是完全错误的。

比较两种译文，不难看出，译文一尽管忠实于原文的意思，但生吞活剥原文的结构，其结果是不听完最后一个字很难知道全句的意思，这无形中增加了听众的压力。相反，译文二采用顺译的方法，并通过增词和词类转换的手段，前后连接，干脆利落，层次分明，地道通顺。类似的例句如下。

(2) The old idea that anyone with a little money can start a business and operate it successfully is no longer valid. (同位语从句)

译文一：那种认为任何人只要有一点钱就可以创业并且经营得很好的旧观念已经过时了。

译文二：过去有人认为，任何人只要有一点资金就可以成功创业，这种观念已经过时了。

译文三：过去有人认为，任何人都可以白手起家，这种观念已经过时了。

译文一生硬拖沓；译文二通顺地道；译文三简洁流畅。

(3) At our party conference last year I said the task to change the national attitude of mind was the most challenging to face for any British Administration since the war. (动词不定式短语作定语)

译文一：在我们去年的党大会上我说过，改变国民思想态度的任务对战后任何一届英国政府来说都是最富挑战性的。

译文二：在去年的党大会上，我曾经说过，我们所面临的任务就是要改变国民的态度。这项任务十分艰巨，是战后历届英国政府都未曾遇到的。

译文一佶屈聱牙，生搬硬套。译文二采用断句增补的方法，自然流畅，一气呵成。

(4) More than 2,000 entries are submitted each year in the Pulitzer Prize competition, and only 21 awards are normally made. The awards are the culmination of a year-long process that begins early in the year with the appointment of 102 distinguished judges who serve on 20 separate juries and are asked to make 3

nominations in each of the 21 categories.（第二句中含有两个定语从句）

译文一：每年有超过 2000 件入选作品参加普利策奖的竞争，但通常只颁发 21 个奖项。这些奖项是长达 1 年过程的终结。它始于每年年初，受委派的 102 名杰出的评审员分成 20 个评审团，在 21 个项目中各提名 3 件作品。

译文二：每年都有 2000 多件作品角逐普利策奖，但通常只设 21 个奖项。评奖过程为期一年，从年初开始。共有 102 位著名的评委，分成 20 个小组，要求他们在 21 大类中各推举 3 件作品。

译文一是典型的死译，是穿着汉语外衣的英语。译文二既忠于原文的意思，又通顺流畅。两相比较，孰优孰劣，不言自明。

汉语长句多见于政论和科技文章，总的原则依然是顺译，同时，根据实际情况，灵活变通。如：

（1）香港回归后，将继续保持自由港的地位，继续发挥国际金融、贸易、航运中心的作用，继续同各国各地区及有关国际组织发展经济文化关系。

After the return, Hong Kong will retain its status of a free port, continue to function as an international financial, trade and shipping center, and maintain and develop its economic and cultural ties with other countries, regions and relevant international organizations.

（2）一些希腊的哲学家们认为，一切物质都是由四种元素构成的，即土、火、空气和水。于是，很多人就认为，如果把这些元素重新组合的话，一种物质就可能变成另一种物质。

Some Greek philosophers held that all matter was made up of the same four "elements" —earth, fire, air and water; and many people therefore thought that if these elements could be rearranged, one substance could be changed into another.

十四、语态转换

英语中被动句的使用比较广泛，而汉语中主动句的使用则比较普遍。因此，在翻译过程中，应根据两种语言在语态方面的差异，进行适当调整，以期符合两种语言的行文特点，使译文更加地道自然。

汉语被动句往往含有"负面"的意思，如不愉快、不如意等。因此，使用起来应十分小心。相反，英语被动语态则无此禁忌，或褒或贬或中性，使用范围不受限制。因此，英译汉时，切忌对号入座，盲目照抄照搬原文结构。

1. 英语被动句在绝大多数情况下可以译成汉语主动句。

比较下列例句两种不同的译法，不难看出，前者生硬死板，后者流畅自然。

（1）I went to the office and was told that the meeting was cancelled.

a. 我到了办公室，被告知会议取消了。

b. 我到了办公室，得知（获悉）会议取消了。

(2) He was promoted to be the CEO of the Haier Group.

a. 他被提拔为海尔集团首席执行官。

b. 他荣升海尔集团首席执行官。

(3) This book has been translated into twenty languages.

a. 该书已被译成二十种语言。

b. 该书已经译成二十种语言。

(4) And this will be dealt with in the next chapter.

a. 这一点将在下一章被讨论。

b. 这一点将在下一章讨论。

(5) Professor Smith is known to us for his great achievements in the study of nanotechnology.

a. 史密斯教授被我们大家所熟知，他在纳米技术研究方面成绩斐然。

b. 史密斯教授我们大家都很熟悉，他在纳米技术研究方面成绩斐然。

(6) According to the regulations, foreign tourists are not allowed to take objects out of China for other people.

a. 根据规定，外国游客不被允许为他人将物品带出中国。

b. 根据规定，外国游客不得为他人将物品带出中国。

2. 下列英语特殊结构可以译成汉语中的无主句。

It is said that... 据说……

It is reported... 据报道……

It is hoped that... 希望……

It is estimated that... 估计……

It must be admitted that... 必须承认……

It is well known that... 众所周知……

It is thought that... 人们认为……

It is suggested that... 建议……

It must be remembered that... 必须记住……

3. 特定情况下一定要译成被动语言，尽量减少"被"字的使用，代之以地道的汉语表达方式。常常用来替换"被"字的词或词组有"挨""遭""遭到""使""为……所""受到"等。

(1) They were frequently beaten and were forced to live in prison-like conditions.

他们经常挨打，被迫在监牢般的环境中生活。

(2) In that case, even if your credit card is stolen, your money is still there.

这样，即使信用卡失窃，你的钱依然完好无损。

(3) The enemy submarine was crippled.
敌人的潜艇受到重创。
(4) The United States had been known as a melting pot.
美国素有"大熔炉"之称。
(5) Many books, like Follow Me, Family Album, USA, are well received.
很多书，如《跟我学》《走遍美国》，都很受欢迎。
(6) He was not swayed by her good looks.
他不为其美貌所动。
4. 汉语中的无主句可以译成英语被动语态。
(1) 办公楼内禁止吸烟。
Smoking is not allowed in the office building.
(2) 此处要建造一座80层的金融中心。
An eighty-story financial center will be built here.
(3) 苏里南说什么语言？
What language is spoken in Surinam?
(4) 冬天必须保证充足的煤炭供应。
A sufficient supply of coal should be guaranteed in winter.
(5) 在解决海洋问题时，不仅要考虑相邻两国的眼前利益，也要考虑到该地区的长期利益。
Consideration should be given to both the immediate interests of two neighboring countries, but also the long-term interests of the whole region in dealing with the sea issue.
(6) 最后，必须指出，保护环境人人有责。
Finally, it must be pointed out that it is everybody's responsibility to protect the environment.
5. 汉语中以泛指性主语为开头的句子可以译成英语被动语态。
(1) 人们常说，熟能生巧。
It is often said that practice makes perfect.
(2) 有人认为，联合国这个名字是由美国总统富兰克林·D·罗斯福提出来的。
The name "United Nations" is thought to have been put forward by US President Franklin D. Roosevelt.
(3) 人们普遍认为，孩子的成长需要营养，同样也离不开鼓励。
It is generally accepted that a child is fed by milk and praise as well.
(4) 众所周知，花生一开始是喂猪的。
It is well known that peanuts were first used as pig feed.

十五、正反变通

正反变通是非常重要的翻译方法,无论是汉译英,还是英译汉,都是如此。理由很简单。同样一句话,可以正说,也可以反说。比如,Staff Only 在不同场合有不同的翻译。如果是超市电梯门或者厕所门上的标识语,可以直译成"员工专用"。如果是商场、图书馆等其他场合的标识语,则可以反译为"顾客止步",这样更符合汉语的习惯。同样,"小心地滑"(商场)"下雨路滑"(高速公路)"油漆未干"等警示语,也可以用反译的方法,使之更符合英语警示语的行文方式。因此,可分别译成"Wet floor""Wet road"和"Wet Paint"。有时,根据不同的上下文或译入语的行文习惯,只能进行正反变通,否则,译文便佶屈聱牙,难以达意。比如,criminal police 不是"犯罪警察"而是"刑警"。同样,riot police 不是"暴力警察",而是"防暴警察"。上述两个例子充分说明,反译法有时是必须的,否则,必然造成错译误译。为了更好地说明问题,请看以下例句。

(一) 英译汉

(1) I couldn't agree more.
我举手双手赞成。

(2) This sort of situation highlights a critical weakness in the ANC leadership: accountability.
这突出地反映了非国大领导人一个极其严重的弱点,即玩忽职守。

(3) With a century of twists and turns behind us, it is not surprising that there is uncertainty in both the United States and China about the future of our responsibility.
过去的一百年并非一帆风顺,难怪美中两国对未来关系的走向都心存疑虑。

(4) This attitude provides a firm foundation that will support the relationship despite tremors and storms.
这种态度为两国关系奠定了坚实的基础,使之能够经受住狂风骤雨的考验。

(5) Your exhibits are very attractive, though the workmanship is not so desirable.
贵方的展品颇有吸引力,不过,工艺还有待提高。

(6) I promise I will become a Chinese expert in no time.
我保证很快就会成为中国通。

(7) They made the fire within no small difficulty.
他们费了好大的劲儿才把火生了起来。

(二) 汉译英

(1) 你已经不小了,知道这种场合该怎么做了。
You are old enough to know what to do on such an occasion.

(2) 问题依然存在。

The problem remained unsolved.

(3) 回家的路上别忘了替我把信寄出去。

Remember to post the letter for me on your way home.

(4) 加倍小心。

You can never be too careful.

(5) 中国如此，世界也不例外。

What is true of China is also true of the world.

(6) 美国素有"大熔炉"之称，因为很多人的祖先是移民。他们来自世界各地，在这片新大陆上定居。

The United States is known as a melting pot because many of its people are descendents of settlers who came from all over the world to make their homes in the new land.

(7) 听说在美国能赚大钱，而且有宗教自由和政治自由，世界各地的人们蜂拥而至，来到美国。

Attracted by reports of great economic opportunities and religious and political freedom, immigrants from all over the world flocked to the United States.

十六、随机应变

掌握了所有"对策"，并不代表可以顺利完成任务，关键在于临场发挥，随机应变。这种能力需要在大量的实践活动中"养成"，即平时加强训练，在大量练习中将口译技能融会贯通，更要注意多积累各方面的知识，加强复述能力，处乱不惊，始终保持平衡心态。知识积累和心态平衡对于同声传译来说，尤为如此。以下例证主要从这两方面强调了随机应变能力的培养。

(1) 下面是笔者的一次亲身经历。

某政府官员在推销自己城市的旅游业时，是这样说的：

大力发展旅游业……（接下来是毫无原因的停顿）

因为是同声传译，笔者马上译为 To promote tourism in（城市名）。此时，该官员如梦方醒，突然说道：

……的目的是……

如果是交替传译，不会成为任何问题，可以等句子完整后再译，比如：

The aim / goal /purpose/ target of promoting tourism in... is...

然而，同传不允许你从头来过。那怎么办呢？此时，平时的积累就起着关键的作用。笔者当时灵机一动，很自然地用了 is aimed to/at 这个短语，故整个句子变成了

To promote tourism in ... is aimed at...

当然，除了这一表达方式之外，还可应用 is targeted to 等。其他场合表示"目的"，还可以用 is intended for、is designed for、seeks to 等。这再次说明"台上一分钟、台下十年功"的说法包含着多少辛苦、多少磨炼。

（2）再举一个例子：中央政府大力支持这个计划。

句子中"大力支持"，既可以用动词（strongly）support 来翻译，也可以用动词短语来翻译，如 give (full / strong) support to，还可以用介词短语 in support of 或形容词短语 supportive of 译之。也就是说，译者可以根据具体情况，灵活选择。

换言之，对于一个出色的译员来说，任何一句话都应有两种或多种表达方式。唯有这样，才能临阵不乱，从容自若。

（3）下面列举几个实例，供初学者参考。

A. 天无绝人之路。

There is always a way out.

Heaven never seals off all exits.

Every cloud has a silver lining.

Heaven will always leave a door open.

B. 近水楼台先得月。

It is always easy to fetch water when the river is near.

First come, first served.

A waterfront pavilion gets the moonlight first.

A baker's wife may bite of a bun, a brewer's wife may bite of a tun.

C. 优点和缺点（利弊）

strong points and weak points

strengths and weaknesses / shortcomings / drawbacks

advantages and disadvantages

merits and demerits

D. 我请客。

It's my treat.

It's on me.

Let me pay.

I'm paying.

I'm treating.

I'm treating you.

I got it.

I'll get it.

Let me treat.

Let me pay the bill.
Let me foot the bill.
I'll pick up the tab.
Let me treat you.
I want to treat.
I want to treat you.
Let me buy you lunch.
Don't say a word. Next time you can pay.